Fellini

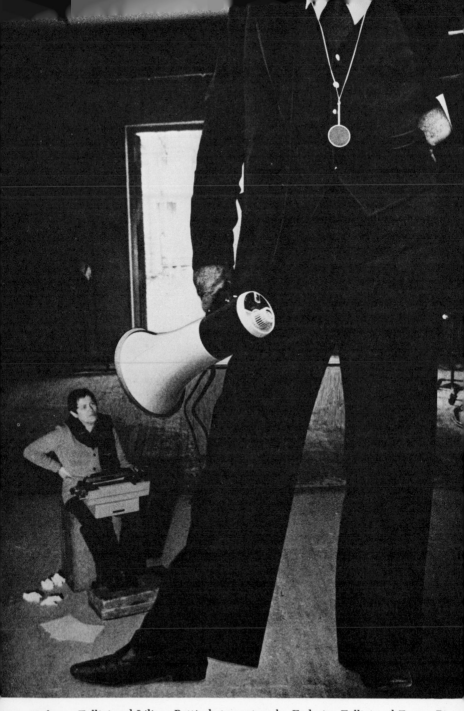

Federico Fellini and Liliana Betti photomontage by Federico Fellini and Franco Pina

Fellini

by
Liliana Betti

Translated from the Italian by Joachim Neugroschel

LITTLE, BROWN AND COMPANY   BOSTON   TORONTO

FIRST ENGLISH LANGUAGE EDITION

LIBRARY OF CONGRESS CATALOGING IN PUBLICATION DATA

BETTI, LILIANA.
FELLINI.

TRANSLATION OF FEDERICO FELLINI.
1. FELLINI, FEDERICO.
PN1998.A3F32413   791.43'0233'0924   79-12360
ISBN 0-316-52786-6

MV

Designed by D. Christine Benders

*Published simultaneously in Canada
by Little, Brown & Company (Canada) Limited*

PRINTED IN THE UNITED STATES OF AMERICA

Fellini

1

The Suitcase

I CAME TO ROME five years ago from a large ugly place in the province of Brescia. I was twenty-two years old and chock-full of mistaken but very precise ideas about myself and what I wanted to do. My arrival in the capital and my early life here were in no way typical or classic. I didn't scrape by on odd jobs, I didn't skip meals, I didn't knock on countless doors that wouldn't open. Federico Fellini was in Rome, and I had come to see Federico Fellini. The whole business wasn't all that easy or quick. My visit to Fellini was preceded by over a year of friendly correspondence, launched by a conviction I had, which was very solid but nourished by air: I wanted to make movies, I wanted to be a film director.

My first letter started with an aphorism by Lawrence Durrell: "We always seek rational reasons for believing in the absurd." At the time, I felt very enthusiastic about it, even though I can't quite ferret out its meaning anymore. At any rate, I promptly received a warm and charming reply from Fellini, saying I had aroused his interest and he would like to meet me. I mention this detail only because everything that happened afterward was due to a fortunate misjudgment. I thought that Fellini's answering me was something extraordinary, I unhesitatingly regarded it as a sign of destiny, I took a headlong plunge and never stopped. Eventually, I came to realize that the only letter-writers who pique Fellini's curiosity and with whom he corresponds punctually are the oddest, the weirdest, in a word, the craziest people.

Within a short time, I sent Fellini an avalanche of letters; mine was a real epistolary delirium. On the other hand, Fellini's letters, when they weren't telegraphic (and they usually were), were warmhearted, impatient reprimands for the dizzying and really gratuitous intellectuality of my texts, which he said "would have made Freud's head whirl."

He made me promises which, when the time came, he went back on with a fatalistic regret that was flattering, but still ironic.

I responded harshly, with the impetuous aggressiveness that's possible only when you don't know someone personally. He made other vague promises.

I left for Rome. He received me with these exact words: "But why didn't you come sooner?"

Like all people who, because of their charisma, are pampered but who are yet not hardened by it, Fellini, in the area of human relationships, allows himself to be overwhelmed by others. If that really is inappropriate, he resists domination or, even better, avoids it.

In slightly more than a year of correspondence, I had at least pinpointed that character trait of Fellini's, something that's often caused disappointment and resentment unless there's immediate recognition of and immediate immunity to this behavior. The disappointment and resentment are rapidly dispelled by Fellini's charm and his skillful system of explanations and justifications — only to recur or else give way to a steady distrust.

Fellini respects feelings, emotions, gut-level preferences, de-

llini with Liliana Betti in the sound studio

sires, moods only if they are spontaneous. And he usually reacts with a commitment that is sincere but that is as ephemeral as its causes. Thus, he acts without involvement toward people, events, things. Unfortunately, he's one of those men of whom a constant deep commitment is required — either because his work puts him right in the middle of a dense network of relationships, or because his personality gathers instinctive support and trust even when he doesn't consent outright to privileges and demands. Now Fellini has never gotten himself into serious trouble or had any really grave incidents, and he ultimately owes this to the fact that his uninvolvement is altogether more active and generous than a mediocre commitment. For he is a good person, who is profoundly interested in, and truly enjoys dealing with, other people.

Protected by the immunity I mentioned earlier, and enclosed in my timidity as in a crystal cube, I underwent a kind of apprenticeship that lasted six or seven months. Fellini is very slow to focus on a feeling, a rapport; he first has to develop the proper climate, an almost physical familiarity.

I spent the early part of this novitiate hard at work in the darkness of a small recording studio, where they were adding the soundtrack to 8½. The excitement over the film, the amazement at the vaguely magical aura around every cinematic operation of Fellini's, even the most technical, the enthusiasm for the daily discovery of Fellini himself — all these things were so overwhelming, that in my efforts to halt them, my clumsiness reached a point of almost physical paralysis. Silently curled up in the depth of an armchair, immersed in a stony immobility for hours, I must have looked like a strange, docile object to anyone who saw me. Every so often, Fellini interrupted my blissful, ecstatic equilibrium with his lively and tactile effusions, those affectionate outbursts for both women and men — hugs, squeezes, kisses. For the docile object, they were catastrophic. I blushed so furiously that I was forced to stick my head in the next armchair, doggedly hunting something. Or else I peered into my purse for an off-the-cuff check of its contents. A mute raptus of wild, untimely gestures, some of them quite indecipherable, swallowed me up like a whirlpool.

Fellini, with the pushy curiosity that is always halfway between the tenderness of a Samaritan and the scornful cruelty of
a slave driver, would speak to me, question me, ask my opinion. I answered in monosyllables or else with an embarrassed
grin, which persisted for no apparent reason, making me look
feeble-minded. Then, at home, I was seized with my insatiable
craze for writing, and I diligently composed notes, letters,
memoranda.

Once 8½ was done, I began meeting Fellini for long drives
that often concluded as follows. He would drop me off, like a
valise, in ever new and unfamiliar areas of Rome, from which I
emerged by hook or crook. And that was how I got to know the
city.

At the end of this singular apprenticeship, Fellini invited me
to stay on with him.

2

The Chauffeur

In the pauses between films, I was Fellini's secretary. During
the preparation and shooting of a film, I acted as an assistant
director or press attaché. And my fourth job, on top of the first
three, was as Fellini's chauffeur.

Characteristically, this last duty, which I performed more
ably than the others, was the one I was most crazy about. It's
easy to guess why. The little Fiat 600, which Fellini presented
to me and which we drove around in during those years, was an
environment in which I daily got to know him better.

All in all, Fellini lives almost exclusively in Rome, frequent-
ing the same places for years now, and always seeing the same
people. And yet for all that, he seems like a traveler you catch
between trains. Even when he's at home with Giulietta and
they're entertaining friends, he has that precarious air of being a
guest himself.

Throughout a given day, he has to face so many people, situations, places, problems, encounters, that any other man would be exhausted and stupefied. But not Fellini. And not so much because this daily whirlwind is the natural outlet for an enormous energy, but more because this hectic existence, which luckily is buoyed up by a tremendous vitality, is the only way he can survive. Furthermore, Fellini is a lazy man, he has no interests aside from filmmaking, he has no hobbies whatsoever, he doesn't like traveling, going to movies or plays, or partying. So it's obvious that a good portion of the events crowding his day have only a dynamic value, they are not ends in themselves. That is to say, they are fairly superfluous.

Fellini has become a past master at effortlessly orchestrating the twelve hours he faces every morning. These hours are a dizzying swarm of deeds, persons, meetings, from which he only steals the time reasonably needed for work or friendship or curiosity. It is precisely in this rigorous, quasi-hygienic respect of necessity as a fruitful yardstick for his time that Federico manages to cope with the fear and anxiety endlessly driving him. And indeed, he copes with them in both material and salutary terms. If he were to slow down the daily rhythm of his life or if he actually had to halt it altogether, there would be a blockage, a paralysis, and he would be totally overwhelmed.

Many people wonder why, for Fellini, life and work are so identical. Others wonder how and when Fellini dedicates himself to a film he wants to make, when he thinks about it, since he never visibly reserves any particular occasions or periods for conceiving his projects. There is only one answer, because the problem is unique. Fellini's day is strewn with buoys, and swimming from one buoy to the next is the only way he can stay afloat. The gaudy plethora of events with which his days are intertwined is the only possible way for his days to exist and for Fellini to bear up under, and live through, them. The indispensable exhausting discipline allows him to conquer that calm and silent space, that relative freedom from himself, in which he can go back over them creatively.

It is often said that when you are with Fellini, even with the best relations of interest, warmth, enthusiasm, you always feel that one part of him is somewhere else, far away, in a place where he is alone and out of reach. For more sensitive people, this can be slightly frustrating. And yet such people ought to realize that Fellini's continual elusiveness is merely the very unfrustrating equivalent of the distinct blocks of solitude and concentration that others prefer to slice out of their time. Fellini's constant delicate margin of liberty requires uncompromising mental gymnastics, which are so compulsive as to appear a bit comical.

It's hard to locate the roots of the anxiety and nervousness that urge Fellini on in his perennial flight. "I can't get myself to sit in a movie house for more than ten minutes, because at a certain point I get impatient, I start to wonder what's happening on Corso Umberto or Piazza Indipendenza, and finally my curiosity gets the better of me, I jump up and leave the theater."

Although my sense of observation is rarely active and almost never fervid, I've so often noticed that reality, no matter how banal, reaches Fellini with a vital, abnormal charge, and his receptivity in such confrontations is habitually altered, expanded, vulnerable. For a thinker or a scientist, reality is the object of an intermediate approach with the resources of intellectual or scientific inquiry. But for an artist, the immediate contact with reality is like a sort of combustion; it is the crucial primal experience, hence extreme, perilous, or neurotic. For Fellini, the most innocuous details of the most familiar reality always cause a gigantic echo. Their tension is so alive that no one else could stand it for long. The resulting anxiety (or alarm) is a kind of immunizing antibody that drives Fellini to seek his own salvation and equilibrium in the constant alternation of diverse realities.

I hope that these off-the-cuff remarks have at least made clear that the provisional is the only thing assuring Fellini a relative détente and serenity, that it is the most beneficial atmosphere, the one in which he is most himself. And since there is nothing more provisional than a drive from one place to another within the city, or a trip from Rome to Fregene and back, my chauf-

feuring was the most authentic and most favorable contribution
to my relationship with Fellini.

All this merely testifies once again that it's much easier for
him to relax with something unimportant or different, for instance, a drive in an automobile. His curious tendency to have
several actions coexisting, his gift for living on multiple levels at
once, are likewise ways for him to try to stay at an ideal point of
equilibrium, the only possible place where he won't be overwhelmed by one thing or another.

The word "driver" may be misleading. Fellini is certainly not
a person who needs a driver in the conventional sense of the
term. For him, "driver" simply means someone sitting next to
him when *he* is at the wheel. Fellini is never alone, for the very
human reason that by himself he can't succeed in being alone.
Solitude would depress him so greatly that it would no longer
be beneficial to his mind, it would turn into an agonizing limbo.

At the wheel of a car, he has amazingly quick reflexes, he
goes the wrong way on one-way streets, and he carries out ma-
neuvers that would terrify the most reckless drivers — for instance, by shooting down a yellow lane ("C'mon, let's pretend
we're a bus!"). All in all, his driving is open-minded but not
foolhardy. Once, I had the bad idea of describing it as a con-
formist's imprudence, and he was offended. He also is totally
unaware of the most elementary needs of the motor. He drives
along for dozens of kilometers in second gear, completely
forgetting to shift into the higher gears, or else he abruptly
switches to low gear while doing fifty kilometers an hour in a car
with manual transmission. And he is capable of long, bloodthirsty discussions, attempting to provide a rational justification
and necessity for some gut-level preference.

If ever anyone else happens to be at the wheel of the car,
with Fellini as a mere passenger — then the fat's in the fire.
Fellini becomes an unbearable pest, the worst kind of backseat
driver, showering the poor victim with recommendations, ex-
hortations, suggestions, accusations, nervously jumping about,
perilously threatening the driver's attention and transmitting a
mortifying suspicion about his ability, and even thrusting him-

self behind the wheel. Then again, Fellini is subject to inexplicable attacks of conservatism. He blindly entrusts himself to professional chauffeurs, and he is basically leery of women drivers.

As I said at the start, a car drive makes Fellini relaxed, sincere, confident, it stirs up his memories and reinvigorates his imagination. This type of vagabondage is certainly the most fruitful way of meeting the people he works with. The recurrent goal of one of his routes is Ostia: "It's like Rimini, but a transfigured Rimini, invented, aseptic, that is to say, without the emotional block of the real Rimini. And then Ostia is so irrevocably ugly that you feel safe, carefree, protected, you can't possibly expect anything worse."

3

The Secretary

UNFORTUNATELY, MY FUNCTION as a secretary during those years was elusive and fluctuating, and it certainly had little to do with what that job normally entails.

The reasons for my daily professional unreality were manifold. First of all, the agenda for a day in Fellini's life is mainly given over to the unforeseen, to unexpected whims or wishes. Second, an encounter or event, for Fellini, consists chiefly in the pleasure of organizing it or bringing it about. Third, a good chunk of Fellini's daily activity has no tangible, concrete necessity, so that the figure of a traditional secretary would merely provide a frivolous or even comical alibi for a psychological climate. Fourth, Fellini's memory is a kind of electronic storehouse, which registers and holds on to data, never communicating it to the person who is supposed to register and store it. The fifth reason is simply one of destiny, the fateful compendium of the first four reasons: I belong to that species of women who are the very opposite of a perfect secretary. I'm disorganized, careless, easily distracted, and my memory scarcely ever asserts itself.

Zeal, feverish goodwill, overactiveness, in general any behavior tending to alter the natural rhythm of things irritates and annoys Fellini. At worst, he responds with silence, and at best with a superficial, deceptive benevolence.

On the other hand, he finds lies highly entertaining, particularly if he can promptly detect them and secretly observe their catastrophic development, just as a simple algebraic problem can have an exhilarating effect on an expert in the subject.

One morning, for example, my zeal got the best of me, and I provoked a double disaster by telling a lie.

The hunt for a space to prepare a new film had been going on for about a month. Absolutely static periods alternated with days of frantic but ineffective on-the-spot investigations all over Rome. Now things were getting urgent, we had to come up with something soon, and the urgency gave me an unjustified sense of guilt, provoking the weird mess that followed.

That morning, Fellini and I were driving over to inspect an apartment on Via Zanardelli, which we had tracked down through a newspaper ad. All at once, without being asked or even slightly consulted, I blurted out an absolutely bare-faced lie. I said that on the previous day I had seen two apartments, one on Via Palestra and the other on Via Nazionale, but I felt that neither was right for our needs. I hoped my statement would remain within the limits of expressing my goodwill and simultaneously indicating how hard it was to find a satisfactory place. But Fellini promptly showed keen interest in the place on Via Nazionale. He said he liked the street, it was ideal for preparing the kind of movie he wanted to make. Via Nazionale was the first street he had seen upon arriving in Rome, and it thus represented, in his fantasy world, the street of transplanting one's roots, entering the unknown, living in isolation. These were just the right moods for the psychological atmosphere of the new film.

He meticulously asked about the details. He wanted to know

exactly where the place on Via Nazionale was located, how many rooms it had, what those rooms were like, what floor it was on, whether there was a telephone. My answers were suspiciously vague and indecisive, and I was so anxious to talk Fellini out of it that when I had to describe the premises, I unhappily went too far and said they were pretty decrepit. Fellini was amazed that there could be a place like that on such a central thoroughfare. So much for that. I was relieved inside, but not fully at ease. The less believable a thing is, the more attractive and plausible it sounds to Fellini. We inspected the apartment on Via Zanardelli without concluding anything. I knew that Fellini had an appointment at eleven, and it was now ten of. All at once, he decided to visit the place on Via Nazionale. At this point, a sensible person would have made a clean breast of things. But unfortunately, my common sense was irremediably paralyzed and compromised by the feeling of being stuck in a mess. Excessively calm and cool, I turned the car and headed for the lion's den. We parked near Piazza Esedra and began the grotesque hunt for a nonexistent office.

After a great deal of confusion going up and down the left side of the street, Fellini, amused and out of patience, asked me head-on: "Listen, Liliana. If you've been doing a number on me, then say so. Nothing serious has happened, it just turned out badly for you." Deeply offended, I replied that the office I had seen was on this street, I was sure of it. So on we went.

Almost placated by my ill-founded certainty, I kept repeating like an automaton that the outside door of the building was small and green. We did come across a door like that, but, just fancy, that was not the one. In a facetious pause, not at all inconceivable in such situations, I timidly hazarded that I may have been daydreaming, for all I knew. I was sort of hoping to exhaust Fellini's insatiably ferocious doggedness by offering an explanation that might strike him as cogent. Nothing doing. We kept striding up and down the sidewalk, and finally the absurd pantomime was over, with a whimper, as if the unleashed tension had been consumed and would not permit any further developments unless I dropped dead.

I admitted telling a lie and being driven by a brutal panic.

Fellini, with the cruelty, tenderness, and sympathy of an impenitent liar, laughed his head off at the sight of my total defeat and my sulky, childish abashment.

Only very recently has Fellini's prodigious memory had sporadic problems; he's been bothered by some troublesome lapses. The first few symptoms of this anomaly elicited his vague surprise, then a slight alarm. Then he tried taking some concrete precautions. After various consultations and discussions, he decided it was high time for me to get a calendar, a book for listing names, appointments, phone numbers, messages, if not for efficiency's sake, then at least for the outer propriety of my job.

But I still don't possess an appointment book. Not only that, but my attempts involving some sort of notebook (I would diligently enter everything, but then forget I had entered it) had such a disastrous outcome that the use of an agenda would have irreparably and officially confirmed my inadequacy.

The opening of the small office on Via della Fortuna at first alarmed me. I was afraid it would force me to follow a precise schedule. But Fellini was as tactful and sympathetic as ever, and his efforts to relieve my fears were so generous that, probably because of his concern, the office lasted only a few months.

All business is handled in such a way that even a relative economic reversal is equally flowing and fortuitous. When I am not working as assistant director in some movie company (which permits me to get along while being an irregular and irregularly paid secretary), Fellini only asks me if I need money. At first, my timidity at expressing anything of the sort was made superfluous by Fellini's initiative. But gradually I became a bit less timid, while Federico became less solicitous and attentive. Two months ago, when I was in bad economic straits, I didn't come to the office for four days. My perhaps brutal but reasonable protest was that I wasn't coming because no one paid me. Fellini was extremely surprised and upset: "What an odd thing to say. . . ." He was surprised and upset like a man who literally doesn't understand such a protest, which is beyond his frame of reference and yet so simple. This episode finally convinced me that Fellini regards me as a daughter who should consider it natural to work for free, or at least without a fixed salary, in her father's business. And that was why he found my requests impolite and inexplicable.

4

The Telephone

IN GENERAL, Fellini gets up rather early in the morning. During his bath, a certain object enters the scene, an instrument that he will pursue implacably and obsessively throughout the day: the telephone.

To describe what the telephone means to Fellini and how many bad habits, dislikes, and fears are identified and sublimated in it, is a hopeless enterprise. One could write a tome of comparative psychology about it, a shivery Edgar Allan Poe story, an interminable statistical finding. Fellini lives by telephoning, or rather, he telephones in order to live, or else he lives from call to call. Fellini continually calls everyone. Fellini continually calls everyone back. Fellini could call on and on without ever making a film, but he could never make a film without calling. Fellini is gentle by nature, but he would kill for a telephone token. Fellini, so full of integrity, so true to himself, would sell

Liliana Betti, done up by Fellini and Danilo Donati for a special Fellini issue of the French fashion journal *Vogue*.

Fellini on the telephone, doodling

body and soul for a telephone call. Fellini telephones at every moment: while thinking, while talking, while reading, while eating, probably while having sex or while sleeping. Fellini could telephone from any place: underwater, in an operating room, from a prison, on Mount Everest, in a mine . . . and I'm sure he'll telephone from beyond the grave. Fellini telephones without a telephone. Fellini telephones himself.

Coiled up with the telephone apparatus, Fellini looks like a vampire lurking for its victim, an asthmatic gasping for oxygen, a postoperative patient receiving a blood transfusion, a thief staking out his objective, a spy intercepting information, a child struggling with a gigantic ice-cream cone, an innocent man awaiting sentence, a guilty man enjoying an easy acquittal. On the telephone, Fellini draws sustenance and is bled to exhaustion.

5

The Phys Ed Teacher

Fᴇʟʟɪɴɪ's ʙᴀᴛʜ is an alternation of wet phoning, singing, roaring, declaiming: a whole trampling, histrionic exhibition by a man looking forward to the day like a delicious morsel. And after the bath, it's time for massages and gymnastics, with the appearance of Ettore Bevilacqua, the first of the fixed persons in Fellini's daily schedule. Bevilacqua is an ex-boxer, short, thickset, with a big, open, childlike face. A wartime wound left him with a dismal affliction, deafness: an infliction he ingeniously transformed into a picturesque and unmistakable attribute. Most deaf people gesticulate a lot and syllabify their words. In Bevilacqua, gestures and loud singsong have become a highly effective pantomime and diction; they are spirited, poetic, and his stories are expressively precise and unbelievably funny.

Bevilacqua has an excited awe, a religious wonder toward words in general, particularly names, brand names, advertising phrases, foreign expressions. ABBAINO, ANITA EKBERG, OSRAM, LA CASA DEL FORMAGGIO, HOW ARE YOU on Bevilacqua's lips become extraordinary metaphysical sounds. And yet I have always suspected that these rough, insatiable verbal embraces in such a simple and naturally intelligent creature are nothing but enchanting, ferocious grimaces of scorn for human language and its confining inauthenticity. Once, Fellini asked Bevilacqua point-blank:

"What's your favorite word?"

Disoriented, besieged by the echoes of a thousand temptations, he finally said: *"Otto"* (the Italian word for "eight"). What a mysterious verdict!

Bevilacqua alternates his massaging with movie acting (under the name of Rector Boileau). It's easy to tell which movie genre is in favor at a given moment by the disguise that Bevilacqua adopts to be "with it." At this time in history, thick mustaches and unkempt hair are the most obvious hommage to the spaghetti Western. It's not surprising that in dealing with such a character, Fellini ultimately gets up his own camouflage, so that together they look like a pair of comedians à la Laurel and Hardy.

One morning, Fellini was driving his car, and Bevilacqua was following in his own. For over a quarter of an hour, right in the midst of the city traffic, the two men engaged in an incessant and furious gunfight. Federico jerked around, took aim, and fired at Bevilacqua, who fell heavily and agonizingly upon his steering wheel, though not without slamming on his brakes and thus forcing the huge tow truck behind him to screech to a halt each time. Finally, blocked at a traffic light, the truck driver, a big, brawny guy, jumped to the ground and ferociously stomped over to confront Bevilacqua about this incredible, dangerous pantomime. At the sight of the ex-boxer's blissful mustachioed mug, the man's fury instantly became a hysterical, whining rage: "Ya gotta mustache! And ya still playin' games!"

Bevilacqua, annoyed, but also flattered since the annoyance derived from a complicity with Fellini, retorted with a particularly satisfied booming and mimicry: "Whaddaya want? D'ya know who's in fronna me? Fellini, the moviemaker! Fe-de-ri-co

Fel-li-ni! We've been shootin' it out for twenny years, him and me! Whatta ya carryin' on about?!"

It was true. For years, Fellini has had his fun plugging Bevilacqua full of lead, while the masseur/actor feigns a blood-curdling death each time. The burly truck driver could do nothing but take note, and, humiliated, jump back into his truck.

Bevilacqua, dressed up as a Mexican peon, rubs, kneads, squeezes Federico, and then moves on to gymnastics. But things take a surprising turn — to say the least. From the room with the gym equipment, you can hear Fellini's voice militarily scanning: one-two, one-two, one-two. If curious eyes peep into the room, they are greeted with a totally unexpected spectacle. Standing in a corner and frowning, Fellini is staring at his specialist Bevilacqua, who is gasping and steaming with sweat while doing knee-bends, body-bends, twists, rotations. And even the enormous grilled steak that ought to compensate for the energy Fellini uses up in his exercises becomes a fair reward for Bevilacqua.

6

Money

W<small>HEN</small> F<small>ELLINI</small> <small>DOESN'T</small> visit him, then in walks Remo, the barber, all dolled up, with blondish hair, and with a lazy and provocative irony. Remo is another basic person in Fellini's day. To carry out his job of shaving, Remo sticks a magnificent monocle in his right eye, which makes him look like a sinister surgeon. Nearly every day, the two men go through high-level financial operations that are incredibly complicated. The most lucid is something like this: shave, tip, and taxi add up to 3,000 lire. Fellini asks Remo for a loan of 10,000 lire, from which he pays him. This inextricable economic complicity with Remo is exemplary of Fellini's disorder in money matters. He never has any cash on him, and for his daily needs he habitually resorts to checks, which he writes out as absentmindedly as a man courteously signing a postcard. Not infrequently, when making out a check, he simultaneously casts doubt on it with a light-headed and atrocious comment: "I must have already overdrawn at least twice this amount!" Such a statement would have to strike terror in the heart of any scrupulous account-holder. But Fellini's financial brinkmanship — the bank willing — is so elastic and approximate that it often comes close to insolvency.

Moreover, Fellini's relationship to money is more incongruent and peculiar than one could imagine. He does appreciate money, he always knows what and how much he wants. But on the other hand, an absolute detachment, almost an incurable obtuseness, prevents him from developing the intimacy that most people have with money. The carelessness, the light-headedness with which he removes money from his pocket, hands it out, takes it in, talks about it — they testify to his remoteness from the whole issue. It amuses him, like a childhood game of numbers, transactions, passwords. He has no sense of property. Which makes him so astoundingly free and easy with other people's property.

Usually, he pays back any money he owes. But in a few cases, he is irritatingly and unaccountably obstinate about refusing to settle a debt. And one should always watch out when he asks, with false sincerity: "How much do I owe you?" For he is almost always sure to go on more or less like this: "Five thousand lire? Fine. Then give me five thousand more, and I'll owe you ten thousand."

He has a kind of timorous respect for insignificant figures like 5,000 lire, 40,000 lire, 75,000 lire. Perhaps these are fossils of having gone without and wished for things in the days when he had nothing.

He doesn't know the meaning of the word "advance payment." Money he has already received is like something that never existed, and thus he can't understand the present obligations deriving from it.

In conclusion, let me tell about an episode that's worth repeating. It was five o'clock in the morning, and Fellini had just spent a night in the Technicolor building with a lawyer named Mattia, a short, witty, patient man. They went to the San Silvestro post office, where Fellini, ignoring the time, rang up an illustrious magistrate for some legal information. Then he wrote a telegram to let Rizzoli know that he had definitely made up his mind not to show *Juliet of the Spirits* at the Venice Festival. After telling the telegraph operator that the cable was to be rushed, he asked Mattia (with a certainty that he magisterially camouflages with doubt) how much loose change he had on him. Three thousand lire was the answer.

"I've got five thousand. Five and three makes eight thousand. . . . Let's see . . ."

The telegraph man told him a rush cable would cost 9,500 lire. So Fellini said to him: "Never mind. I'll send an ordinary wire."

The man's trancelike stupor violently expressed the paradox of the situation. The explosive content of the telegram would unleash the wildest journalistic battle, and yet the famous nightbird was unable to pay for having it rushed.

7

Mail

FELLINI READS any letter he gets, indiscriminately and with
the impatient curiosity of a man forever awaiting a message, a
bit of information, a revelation that still hasn't come. The first
culling of a bundle of correspondence promptly results in the
destruction of a good half of it. Federico keeps the rest in his
pocket, irresolutely, for a couple of days. The second culling
wipes away half of what's left; and finally, the third culling
reduces the mail to a few pieces, to which he will reply. Often,
therefore, my taking care of the correspondence means watching the spectacle of Fellini tearing up one letter after another.

This uncontrollable destructiveness extends to everything — photos, scripts, newspapers — and Fellini ascribes it to
his "thief's complex," which won't allow him to leave any traces
behind. My feeling is that his destructive lust is part of the
provisional quality that he tries to maintain through the most

ephemeral reality, and it would be corrupted by even the innocent but confining preservation of a few letters. For my part, I follow his example with my own vagueness; I never make or keep copies of any reply, which sometimes causes confusion and embarrassment.

Fellini's mail could be subdivided as follows:

A huge portion consists of invitations from all over the world to festivals, screenings, retrospectives, lectures, panel discussions, symposiums, awards, various ceremonies and events, cocktail parties, banquets, even orgies, summit meetings, private showings, baptisms. If Fellini accepted all of them, he would have to spend the rest of his life in planes, trains, and hotels. A couple of years ago, a New York daily announced that Fellini would be giving a series of lectures in the United States. The false item unleashed a rather comical virus, given the exceptional nature of the contagion: every university and college in America invited Fellini for a visit.

Tokyo. At the moment, for instance, the Japanese capital is the "city of the screen" in its turn. Fellini is using it to safeguard his own freedom. And so Tokyo is the official excuse for turning down every invitation, the major commitment dominating and overwhelming all others. "I have to leave for Tokyo. . . ." "During that time I'll be in Tokyo. . . ." "When I come back from Tokyo. . . ." Fellini thinks that the more remote and exotic the pretext-city is, the more credible and awesome it sounds, so that no one will object. The succession of these places has reached a crescendo, nearly turning Fellini into a restless and insatiable traveler: Hamburg, London, Rotterdam, Rio de Janeiro, Afghanistan, Mexico, Miami Beach, the Fiji Islands, and so many other wild places on the far side of the globe.

This is the way Fellini travels: he makes believe to other people, as though knowing that they picture him in those spots might contribute to creating, at least deceptively, what a natural uninterest and laziness prevent him from doing. In reality, his utterly mysterious, unattainable vagabondage is limited to the triangle of Rome/Fregene/Ostia, with a rare outing to Viterbo.

A further very notable part of Fellini's mail comes from people asking for things: screen tests, work, money, apartments, advice, opinions, travel, wigs, cars, autographs, references, testimonials, or even just a reply. Or else from people offering things: scripts, ideas, patents, advice, opinions, collaboration, insults, threats, a daughter, land, confessions, biographies, love, mysterious anonymous warnings, stamp collections, spiritualist sessions, hospitality, affinity, Lourdes water.

Here are a few examples of letters that Fellini receives daily. The slim and random selection nevertheless reveals the — albeit humble — charm and vivacity of this fantastic literature.

Rome, March 21, 1971

Dear Signor Fellini,

I am a boy, eight years old, and I would like to become a clown, my mother says it's all right, can you give me some information on circuses and the life of clowns?

Thank you.

Best regards from your admirer,

Fernando

(please send me an answer)

Turin, March 13, 1967

I, the undersigned J. M., pay my respects to you and your family. And I beg to inform you that I have written tragedies, comedies, and scenarios, which astonish all the producers and directors of sinema. They are entitled: *Tragical Night in Rome for the Twofold Assassin of the Countess Rebecca.* Who is strangled by the family doctor in the Via Appia Antica, discovered by the chief of the New York secret police, Jean Ringo, a tragedy of tragedies. *Little Butterfly Assassinated in Trastevere. Princess Imperial Violets* who lived twice. *His Enemies Feared Him and A Tsitsi Fly Killed Him. The Oak. The Snake Pit Discovered under Cas-*

*tello Sant'Angelo. Bread, Love, and Melancholy.
The Lady Sniper.* Which would win first prize
even in Vatican City for the great apostolate of the
Sniperess in a tormented Indochina, earning the
palm of martyrdom. *The Palm of Martyrdom for
an American Actress.* These were written by the
undersigned, an ex-monk, son of the poor man of
Assisi.

If you are interested, I am willing to send them
to you in Italian and in English, for the United
States.

J. M.

Brescia, 5/2/1970

My dear Signor Fellini,

I am one of your greatest admirers, I am writing to tell you about a film project that I would
like to propose to you: of course, you could ar-
range it properly. Now this film is about my life.
And I would want to play the lead myself because
I and some of my girlfriends have already tried it
out and it worked marvelously!! And we took in
almost 300,000 lire for the missionaries. I would
be willing to come to Rome, but only if room and
board are included, since my family is not all that
well off. My dad works, but the money goes, and
so I decided to do this in order to earn something
to send home.

I am sixteen, and people say that I'm very cute.
Now this is how I would plan the film: It begins
with my life at home, where I see girlfriends at
school and always come back afraid of my nasty father, who is very quick with his hands with Mom
and bawls me out for coming ten minutes late.
With the fear of seeing my mother killed by my
father.

Then, life at school, which turns out badly be-

cause of a quarrel with the girls I drink bleach and
thus I have to go to the hospital and lose out on
my diploma.

And so my father will send me out to work if I
don't find food and a place to sleep. Here I know
a boy whose family is very rich, and his name is
Paolo, little by little we realize we're in love.

But my dad won't hear of it.

And so I begin to see that he doesn't like me.

And I hate him!!!

But I don't know the ending. That's up to you.

Best wishes,
Maria B.

Freiburg, July 7, 1971

I am turning to you with a rather unusual request:
I would be grateful if you could tell me where the
location shots of the movie 8½ were done and in
what city the station that appears in the film is
located.

My husband is mad about railroads and when
he saw your movie he was so dumbstruck by the
station that he made up his mind to see it first-
hand during summer vacation in Italy.

Hoping to receive a speedy reply, I thank you
very much.

Albertina H.

Varese, September 9, 1968

For thirteen years now I have been subjected
to a disgusting torture and slavery by my hyena of
a mother-in-law and by her super-daughter my
wife. After an infinity of tricks and quarrels she finally refused even the legitimate one with the
atomic mushroom it lessened the reflection of
whoever had to judge it, for which they condemned me to the atrocity of putative spouse; but
now I say that's it and I will fight till the last drop
of blood so as to get rid of her once and for all.

You will certainly translate from harsh reality into a film of international fame for the morale of the male sex facing the famous prepotency of the weaker sex, which is now crushing the stronger sex. And it even came so far after ten years when I didn't come near her, that I was hauled into court to acknowledge a child of mysterious origin, and precisely at this point I boiled over and she was always saying she was pure, decent, and made a model family?????

The film, if you find it's right, will be called *Reality of Love in an Indissoluble Bond*. If you do find it all right, please confirm by telephone, and I am also including postage stamps, and if you do not confirm your interest within thirteen days I am counting until today on your personality and your honor to tear up my gift.

R. C. B.

Subject for Film
Title
I + I = LSD

A young woman; tired of her ordinary life (home and husband), decides, on the spur of the moment, to turn to drugs. One evening when she is alone, she gets drugs from a few friendly dealers; she takes a strong dose and as in a dream undergoes a terrible experience.

She ends up in a science-fiction environment; has relations with an unidentified monstrous being. Halfway between human and animal. This incestuous union (lasting only a few hours) gives birth to a semi-adult creature who is likewise horrible. A creature endowed with murderous strength. Capable of doing terrible things. He brings moral overthrow and the most dreadful death wherever he goes. His frequent orgies are diabolical; almost conceived personally by Satan and his insatiable lust for obscenity. Finally, the mother herself; disgusted by what she has done, she kills him with her own hands. She destroys the lair in which they live; surrounded by a small court of their perverted fellows and disciples, and then she too is killed by falling off a cliff. An apocalyptic earthquake; it closes forever the gate to that mysterious realm of indecency, and no one will ever again see it consciously.

The young woman awakens from her nightmare. Incredulous; she goes through her house seeking the body of her monster-son. But at this point she realizes she imagined everything because of the LSD. When her husband comes home, she doesn't say anything about what happened, and a bit later (after throwing out the drug), she falls asleep Happy; in her marital bed.

THE END

(9/13/69)

P. Maria O.

Providence, Rhode Island
October 17, 1966

Dear Signor Fellini,

I saw you on television together with the producer Joe Levine. During the telecast, you spoke about your career. I too had a career writing for the cinema, I wrote *La Dolce Vita*, *8½*, and other films. But for a long time now, I have not been writing for the movies, I have been ill. To tell the truth, I "drink too much." On TV, you said you never see your scriptwriters, that's true, I've never seen you. I've never gotten even one red cent for writing *La Dolce Vita*, etc., etc. If you want to get in touch with me, write to

Ernest E. G.

Providence, Rhode Island, U.S.A.

The Death of a Hippy

I always remember you dear friend the way they took you away from the street in handcuffs and flanked by two guards.

I always remember you dear friend with your smiling eyes that looked at my furiously red eyes furious for being all alone against so many.

You were neither a thief nor a murderer but they had found a few grams inside your home.

In the morning, there you were in the news, in black and white: *DRUGGED* HIPPY.

In that bizarre trial you were given three much too long years to spend, and you never spent them.

After just a few months in prison, the guard did not see you as usual at the window, opening the door he saw you on the floor in a pool of blood, he turned your body over to feel for your heart, but in vain, your heart was cold and you were dead.

Your death too was written up in the newspaper as an example to all those who have the vice of smoking and all forbidden things.

Just two days ago I met your wife by the river, she was watching the sunset, I said hello how are you, she turned her eyes very slowly they were flooded.

She was was no longer a woman, she was a wraith waiting to *JOIN YOU.*
Death, i fear you no more

Dear Fellini,

Why haven't you or anyone else made a movie on the spinster? i.e. the single woman, unseduced, 32–35 years old? The way she lives, her taboos, etc. Do you have unmarried sisters? Or cousins?

Cabiria, and the character in *La Strada*, Giulietta, etc. have been depicted, but not the single woman — and do not dwell on those who resolve everything by means of free love, but rather on those who are not resigned and yet unable (for so many reasons) to resolve their problem. Make a film in this vein and finally say what you have to: do you men really desire virginity or not? What do you want from a woman? Why is there a sexual (or supposedly sexual) education in one way for the son and total renunciation for the daughter? Why not prepare the parents who then have an unmarried daughter in the house like an affliction (unless the fiancé or even husband is dead, or else the engagement didn't come off). Too much severity, too many demands on the one side; and on the other side, total liberty for the male; and thus we have old maids, sour spinsters, dried-up, wrinkled virgins or "the daughters of some congregation," etc. Are all of them resigned and convinced of their chastity, etc. or do they condemn others for living? In any case, why don't *you* make a film?

In *The Leopard*, it was the "Lampedusa spinsters."

Rome, 3/15/1968

I am a fervent admiress of you and your works, and I have a vocation for acting and am now doing comic parts in various plays, I am not timid, I have a fine pronunciation, I am ready to take on any parts, and I have an excellent figure both from the front and in profile in ancient and modern costumes and two-piece bathing-suits, I am willing to take any roles that you would consider right according to the demands of the script, I entreat you earnestly to give me a screentest. At the same time, I would like to say that I have an ex-

cellent physical appearance, with the following
measurements
Height: m. 1.66
chest: cm. 85
waist: cm. 65
hips: 93
breast (vertical): 12
back of hips (vertical): 20
back of hips (horizontal): 40
legs (length): 81
thighs (circumference): 38
knees (circumference): 33
calf: 31
ankles: 19
length of arm: 57
length of hands: 12
eyes: dark brown
mouth: seductive (that's what they say)
nose: normal, slightly tilted
hair: light brown, length: cm. 70 very thick

Best wishes,
Paola R.

I haven't drunk, on the contrary, I've just had
milk and rice today

Well, you will say, why don't you speak?

The subconscious the matter touches me somewhat closely. They say it depends on sexual dis-
satisfaction, what humbug. I always see myself in
the clothes of Mrs. Masina in that film when she
is miserable while the carnival runs riot, alone
with her misery. *Spychoanalysis* and I will tell
you that you must cure me of everything, there
were two funny films, one by Totò and those by
Ciccio and Franco Ingrassia *Spychoanalysis* Is
there a pain or displeasure that torments you?
Look for the comic side it's like a medicine even

for great men before making any serious decision they would have to see the funny side. Comedy removes the poison from the system. Have you seen the flying saucers with Alberto Sordi? All in the lunatic asylum.

Cordially,
Sabina

Torino, May 15, 1966

Dear Signore Fellini,

I am writing to you for advice concerning my profession.

I am a boy of 25 from Padua, 5'10", blond hair, brown eyes. I feel that you are the only person who can help me. I will come to the point. Since my infancy, I have felt physically and sexually like a woman, at the age of fifteen I obtained my parents' consent to get treatment, since I was more of a woman than a man. Now, after my treatments, I am nearly a woman, the only thing remaining is the operation. I am now working as a photographer's model and my salary is minimal, just enough for my clothes and my food, and believe me, my clothes cost quite a bit, considering the type of work I do, and until now I have not been able to achieve my goal. What I am asking of you is, above all, understanding, and I beg you not to throw out my letter, which is my entire hope. I am asking you, if I may, for a job that could allow me to resolve my all too precarious situation. I am enclosing two photos so that you may see the change I have already gone through. Thank you very much,

Lorenza M.

Dear Signor Federigo Fellini,

I am a fifteen-year-old girl my name is Teodora and you are my favorite moviemaker. I am writing to you because I would very much like to make movies, my granddad had a photoromance I don't know who gave it to him and before dying he gave it to me and said "take it, it will bring you luck." Signor Fellini if you would like to see this photoromance to see whether you like it, let me know and I will send it to you.

Happy New Year,
Teodora

Managing Director's Office Teodora Varese
The romance is titled *Paola*.

Città della Pieve 9/27/1966
Dear Fellini,
This is the first time in thirty years that I am writing to you. YOU ARE WONDERFUL and I am on your side in the litigation with PONTI. Under its veneer of civilization, comprehension, and honesty, the world has moved from the ancient law of the survival of the strongest and the fittest.
(BUT THAT WAS AN ANCIENT LAW)
Today at last a man of courage — BRAVO!
I am on your side because when I had to tell a strong and fit man: You are a *SHIT* I told him and lest he forget it I confirmed it by registered mail.
Between the strong and the fit man and your INTELLIGENCE, your CULTURE, and your EXPERIENCE, the court . . . can only decide in your favor.
They reached agreement right away, the strong and the fit, but I wish that you too would call them a SHIT.
Hugs and kisses to you, out of my deep friendship for you, I have never allowed questions of interest to interfere.

M. D.

Let me give you a small proof of a further vulgar
action of Ponti's . . .
[Editor's note: The litigation mentioned by the
letter-writer was with De Laurentiis, not Ponti.]

                                    Verona 3. 1. 1966
Illustrious thinker,
As an official of the Imperial Court of Vienna
with a mission of delicate political investiture for a
millenary Roman power, I could observe those
movements of cynical oppression, intrigues, dra-
mas, dreadful tragedies, as well as those disconcerting betrayals that the tyranny of the Haps-
burgs makes more horrible and criminal.

Nourished on this bread of life when living between the gaudy walls of the ancient dynasty, it
was possible for me to fill up my notebook with a
whole variety of current events so as to put a large
volume on the balance of light at the proper moment, a volume that would in a serious and docu-
mented way reflect the grand history of those
urgent and ultimate tremors originating in the
cold will of a despot such as Emperor Franz Jo-
seph was all his days.

On his "illuminated" throne he could not
forgive his nephew Archduke Ferdinand for his
morganatic marriage with the Polish countess
Sofia Choteck; he plotted with all the astuteness
of a Pharisee, succeeding in having the high couple fall victim to the Serbo-Croatian conspirators
in the planned massacre, which took place, as we
all know, in that turbulent Sarajevo on June 28,
1914.

Analyzing each separate fact, I had to power-
lessly observe the uproar of the diabolical ma-
chinations, thus finding myself at the center of the
horrible tragedy, at the very instant that the poor

archduke and archduchess were breathing their last.

Then observing the transparency of the pomp and ill fortune, I thought it well to unite in a funeral pyre the criminal moves, including even the most removed particulars so my historical book of over a thousand pages could some day educate the reader to a more and more refined taste, attracting the greatest attention to the personage most responsible for so much butchery.

Considering, thus, the worldwide importance of the historical narrative, illustrious thinkers and dramatists of established fame have overcome my skepticism by encouraging me to take up contact with you alone who as a great artist can comprehend the already demonstrated universality of the work and pour it into a *colossal film.*

The utter potency of dizzying twists requires the stamp of genius, and no lesser artist than yourself could truly interpret the real concatenation of the apparently unconnected demands brought on by the horrifying imperial cataclysms leading to the destruction of the powerful and haughty thrones of Central Europe.

Hoping for a patient share of your attention, may I express my deepest admiration.

Mirella H.

Vicenza, 5-7-66

Dear Signor Fellini,

Please excuse me for taking the liberty of writing these few lines. I need help: I beg you, do not say no, but I need a *wig,* and I can't afford it, I'm too poor. Please try and understand my state of mind and my desperation, and if you can understand me, do not deny me this request, I am certain that with your good heart and soul you will save me from my despair. I simply have to have a WIG and I thank you and I will keep thanking you for the rest of my life. I would like this to remain a secret between the two of us. I thank you with an anxious soul and I send you my very best regards.

Giovanni M.

Please forgive my forwardness:
the color of the hair and the
shape of the head are those of Jonni Dorelli
this is very urgent

(My bottomless thinks)

Modena, June 15, 1971

I am in grade school.

I always go the movies to see your cowboy and Indian movies and I like them so much that I talk about them at school. Now, all we talk about in class is you. I ask you, also on behalf of my friends, if you can send us one of the necklaces worn by the Indian warriors.

We will hang it up in our classroom.

Thanks you,
Alberto

Fellini never says no to anyone, he never turns anything down, he is never specific, detailed, or clear. He merely delays, promises, wavers, and waits.

8

The Truth

I T'S OBVIOUS THAT this practice is not limited to correspondence; it goes through the entire ethics of Fellini's behavior, defining all his relations to other people, and it forms an aspect of him that petty gossip, a conventional and widespread opinion, a certain type of hack journalism have transformed into a legend, sort of monstrous and frivolous at once: Fellini's habit of lying, or rather his habitual and highly personal manipulation of the truth. Naturally, I can't say anything definitive on the subject, but at least I'll try to avoid that fatuous, conspiratorial, or moralistic attitude that this topic always seems to arouse. The first reaction at being confronted with Fellini's mendaciousness is a troublesome disorientation, because his mendaciousness is expressed in an intricate, contradictory, and evasive system of correlations, implications, and results.

Is Fellini an ordinary liar with all the pathological implications? Or is he simply a man eaten alive by his own bent for the fantastic and fanciful and thus incessantly forced to reinvent, to embellish, to distort the facts and experiences of reality? By his very nature, he certainly belongs to the second category. But he also belongs to the first one by the consistent application of that faculty. The liar, then, would be a sort of vulgarized inventor.

I believe that Fellini tells lies for two main reasons.

The first, as I have said earlier, is his weakness or delicacy, which will not allow him to tolerate any discord, discomfort, or disappointment that he himself has caused. In this sense, as he often repeats, his way of lying consists in telling others, or letting them believe, what they want to be told or to believe. I would also have to add that Fellini's pliability is part of his urge always to leave the door open to any development or eventuality, hence granting those who approach him the painful freedom of their needs or illusions.

The second reason is Fellini's desire to conserve and protect the material space and time of his own freedom. In general, this type of liberty is possible either by isolating oneself or by limiting and piloting the liberty of others. And since one of the most affable ways of controlling other people is to tell them lies, Fellini simply defends himself conscientiously with a discreet armor of falsehoods.

At times, Fellini tells completely gratuitous lies, without reason or utility. The vice of lying is like classical ballet: it permits no pauses, relaxation, vacations, it requires a constant and endless training.

The instruments of the successful liar are: quick reflexes, a formidable memory, psychological empathy, and total unscrupulousness. Fellini possesses all four to a prodigious extent.

If anyone touches that key, the key of the liar, Fellini at first is enormously astounded, then he loses patience, and finally goes into a rage, disclaiming any possibility of his ever telling a lie. Even for him, this is the obligatory concession that the liar has to make to his own archetype. To conclude, there's no telling why people are so hostile to liars: if they are not caught, then they're not liars, and if they *are* found out, then they're harmless.

9

Meals

ONE OF FELLINI'S daily problems is to avoid eating alone; it's even better if he has lots of company. As for selecting a restaurant: if he doesn't have a recurrent fleeting crush on a certain place, he follows his whim of the moment (hence one of his mysterious classifications of the restaurants of Rome), or else he goes by the kind of guests he has invited.

However, Fellini's favorite eating-place is Da Cesarina, for the very simple, unrivaled, and absolute fact of Cesarina herself, a huge woman from Bologna, with the aggressive and inscrutable face of Puss-in-Boots, the brusque and at times rude patronly bearing of an Emilian official.

Lunch at Cesarina's is a choice, a perfect act. To call Cesarina a woman is almost useless. Cesarina is a Culinary System, a gastronomical philosophy; her egg custard isn't a dessert, it's a meditation, a Shakespearean soliloquy, a Pythagorean theorem.

A precise description of her kind of woman is not just futile, it's impossible. She is the very embodiment of the concept of a *vivandière,* the idea of a restaurant-keeper. That's why she can't stand having women on her premises: cooking is a female duty and an homage to the male.

Cesarina lives exclusively in her restaurant. Outside, she probably dissolves and takes on a different personality like Dr. Jekyll and his Mr. Hyde.

Fellini maintains that Cesarina has a psychological relationship only to paprika, parsley sauce, and beefsteak Bolognese. Only an artist, a fool, a saint, or scientist identifies himself so completely, so deliriously with the object of his vocation. And Fellini would not be at all surprised if there were a seminar of eminent specialists with Cesarina sitting next to Einstein, Marcuse, Von Braun.

When asked to give her opinion of other eateries, she ignores the provocation, exuding the overbearing reserve of a pope. Her pendulous gait as she comes over to a patron, the serious and attentive air of a person who will not joke because he is performing a kind of religious rite, her quick and incessant moves from table to table, the tempi, the pauses of her sonorous stresses in the Romagna dialect, her sudden and solitary laughter, her disdainful and astonished looks, the compliments she discreetly garners as predictable things — this whole spectacle of gestures and words is so self-contained, so autonomous and so detached from even a minimum need to communicate that Cesarina becomes a literary character radiating good cheer and conquering all hearts on the spot.

In 1938, in Bologna, when Fellini was still very young, Cesarina fed him for four months after first throwing him out of her *trattoria* because he didn't have enough money to pay the check. Now she waits for him every day like a son, a prestigious witness, an artist-colleague.

One evening, Fellini brought Ingmar Bergman to Cesarina's. Fellini has great respect and friendship for the Swedish director and feels somewhat congenial with him, even though he may apply the words "frozen sperm" — with a shiver of strangeness — to the neurotic depth, the hopelessly gloomy at-

Liliana Betti as a vamp, sketched by Fellini on the napkin of a Roman restaurant

Liliana Betti in historical costumes, writing, as Sherlock Holmes, Fred Astaire, and a boxer, sketched by Fellini

Anita Ekberg, drawn by Fellini

mosphere of Bergman's latest film, *The Hour of the Wolf.* "He's very likable," Fellini says about his colleague. "He's like a dentist or doctor. He has a singular face, it's somewhat disquieting, the left eye seems blind, he looks soapy, congealed, like a friend who might suddenly end up in a madhouse for something from which he'll recover right away."

That evening at Cesarina's the two men who can be considered the greatest living moviemakers had an incredible dialogue, worth reporting here. Naturally, it could only be Fellini who directed the dialogue, beckoningly and irreverently. When Bergman asked him about his future work projects, Fellini replied absentmindedly: "I'm preparing a film on death, and I hope to start shooting in a couple of months."

Bergman perked up his ears in keen curiosity. Death is customarily under his jurisdiction. Fellini went on: "About six months ago, I was seriously ill, and I thought —"

Bergman, terrified at losing ground, broke in:

"I was very sick myself a couple of years ago, I really thought I wouldn't make it. . . ."

But Fellini interrupted, patiently but firmly:

"Yes, but I was at death's door. Why, I practically had one foot in the grave. That's why I know everything about death there is to know."

Bergman, gesticulating wildly, pawing the air: "I had an injection once, it causes a kind of clinical death for five hours, and I came to the conclusion that death is simply nonexistence."

Fellini, with polemical doubt: "Five hours strikes me as rather meager for making such a definite statement. You would really have to experience death for at least five years!"

Fellini's impatience at the table is decidedly pathological. No sooner does he order a dish than he expects it to materialize before him (at bottom, magic is simply the temporal materialization of logic).

Since normally this never happens, he hops about nervously between the table and the phone, the table and the kitchen, he keeps making embarrassing demands on the waiter, there is an empty eating of antipastos and fruit, almost half a meal, there is a continuous unreasonable displacement of the silverware and the glasses, there are exhausting and anguished rearrangings of plates, bread, bottles. At this point, the only thing that can neutralize and calm down this chaotic storming is to give Fellini a sheet of paper or else the menu, or simply a napkin. He will instantly begin drawing, sketch after sketch: the caricature of a friend sitting opposite him, the obsessive repetition of an anatomical detail, indecipherable graphic allusions. And in the absorbed frenzy in which he draws, one can detect something more than a pure pastime: an exercise, an attitude for the visible materialization of a feeling, a fragment of a past image, an all-too-haunting specter.

Fellini's lunch is generally highly eclectic; he likes to eat a bit of everything. That's why one should never be taken in by his very kind suggestions as to the choice of such-and-such a dish: he makes sure that the diners have various dishes so that he can pluck out and taste a bit of everything. An absolute preference of his is fish. And he is always amazed at my indecisiveness about his favorite food. One day, after an utter stupor, Fellini asked me point-blank: "Listen, what's your zodiac sign anyway?"

I said it was Pisces; and after a pause, I rather stolidly added: "You mean I ought to like fish, don't you?"

He concluded impassively: "Not necessarily. For instance, I'm a Capricorn, but that doesn't mean I like goat meat."

Fellini's frenzy at assigning places at the table may appear to derive from an intransigent professional deformation: that of the director who stabilizes, decides, organizes. In reality, his mania is merely a device. The objective is a sensible juxtaposition of the diverse temperaments and characters so as to achieve a joyous equilibrium, a kind of mental harmony. When you realize that this harmony is not just for Fellini's personal comfort at the expense of others, but actually creates a fine atmosphere for the entire company — despite the initial discomfort and awkwardness — then the thesis of a professional deformation seems more like a profound vocation than a mere function.

The moment he swallows the last mouthful, Fellini folds up his napkin and starts to fret and fidget in his chair. It's a new period of nervousness, it's already time to go. But where?

10

Women

BRUTALLY ATTACKED by feminists and antifeminists, strenuously interrogated by journalists, tranquilly provoked by psychologists to diagnose, speak, talk about women, about their present situation, about women in his films, about his general attitude toward women, Fellini nearly always begins with this cautious statement: "I have not yet come to understand my relationship to women, to the female body and its rotundities which can assume such fabulous dimensions as to be a moon or a mountain or some mysterious planet. . . ."

It takes a moment to realize that this humble admission is just simple logic: a man to whom female rotundities seem like fluctuating planetary volumes *should* have a difficult time understanding his own relationship to those geological anatomies.

For a public person, such as he is, daily exposed to the attention and curiosity of people, it is nevertheless exceptional that they know nothing about his private stories, relationships, habits, and seasons of the heart. Logically, one would have to conclude that Fellini has no love life, or if he does, then he knows how to defend his "privacy" with diabolical cunning. But any reasonable acquaintance with Fellini makes you realize that both hypotheses are wrong. The discretion attending his emotional commitment is not simply a protective expedient, the manifestation of a style. It actually expresses the deepest meaning, the truest nature of that commitment.

For Fellini, love — though accompanied by an emotional adherence and an unfailing participation of the imagination — is resolved almost internally in sensual ignition and incandescence. In this way, love and work, for him, express an identical mercurial nature, they are episodes liberating vital energy in a pure state. Hence, love and work can scarcely coexist; and if they do coexist, they cannot integrate into a single vital unity.

The love experience for the psychological type of the artist is a means, an extreme opportunity, at the limit of which he approaches the awareness or at least the inkling of various truths and realities that are generally alien to us. Inevitably, an artist is thereby forced to consider women — the instruments of that experience — with the agitated, sacred, and yet brutal respect that always arouses the mind when it assumes a shape. It is no coincidence that this particular psychological aspect vanishes the moment the woman laboriously tries to achieve her own individuality.

Fellini, absorbed in something resembling nostalgia, always says that he has never known romantic love, the kind celebrated by so many poets. And he quickly adds that this is a limit, perhaps a dent left by a Catholic upbringing, which mortifies women in an unnatural dissection of their attributes and functions. However, I believe that this arrested development, this distortion, is to a certain extent grafted on his mode of being. My hypothesis may be naïve or farfetched. But all in all, an artist like Fellini is a very particular kind of human being, perhaps even slightly monstrous.

At times, Fellini's vampirelike craving for female plasma has the cadences of a comical tarantella, greedy and insatiable. On a set, for instance, he appears to avoid slowdowns or breakdowns in his work energy by tirelessly alternating a robust and affectionate hug for the buxom seamstress, a quick, conspiratorial whisper with the performing actress, an instant of solitary curiosity with a newly arrived guest, a fast telephone call about some sort of long delay, then another embrace here, a fondling there, an audacious running quip for his collaborator, a luncheon invitation for a character actress, a tender but brutally intimate question to an old extra. The innocence of this indefatigable ritual is firmly guaranteed by the fact that it is always public, like the effusions of children, and it is frequently performed with the imperceptible distraction of children satisfying their natural needs.

With an analogy that seems to translate a simple and yet singular habit into a destiny, Fellini says: "In my life, I feel as if I were on a stage where everything has already existed from the very start. Even the female characters have been there forever. All I do is put up a floodlight, illuminate a detail, correct a backdrop." This progressive gathering of emotional relationships, their cyclical looming and sinking without ever fading away, according to the demands of a changing equilibrium or an indecipherable filmscript — in short, the maintenance of all these personages in the witchcraft of this private stage, if it's easier and more spontaneous for him, requires a considerable availability and application on Fellini's part: a psychology of surprising elasticity, a mental system of diverse and autonomous relays permitting him to pass from one atmosphere to another with no residues or aftermaths and to live through each different moment with an absolutely sincere intensity. And then, a dose of guile and cynicism, forgivable to the extent that the tenderness, generosity, or need for self-defense and salvation, which causes those traits, is authentic. Thus, someone may whisper an anxious question over the telephone: "Do you miss me?" And Fellini, that knowing and involuntary swindler, answers with an unrivaled and obscurely meaningful phonetic ambiguity: "Sooooo buch!" Or else, to keep up a past complicity or nourish the illusion of a possible new start, he may even feign an indulgent physiological affinity: "Why, last night, at the very

Claudia Cardinale in 8½

Fellini with Marcello Mastroianni and Sophia Loren on the set of 8½

nouk Aimée and Sandra Milo in 8½

Anita Ekberg in *La Dolce Vita*

8½, Fellini showing Mastroianni how to do it

Cigarette break in 8½

Marcello Mastroianni as Guido in 8½

same time, I also had a terrible attack of bile, I was sick all night long!"

In a recent interview, Fellini said: "The true value of women or men and the meaning of their encounters or their reciprocal emotions, like all other things, take on a real and profound significance for me when the lights go on on the set. There, everything enraptures me, everything is clear, intelligible. Off the set, everything confuses me, and I can't make any judgments, state any opinions."

Apart from my personal, deep-rooted suspicion that this gap doesn't really exist (life for Fellini is a gigantic, tumultuous set), it can't be as neat as he claims. One thing that has always struck me about Fellini is his faculty for letting his emotional interest in and attraction to a woman coexist with a diagnostic lucidity, a critical aloofness, the basis of which is always and primarily a sense of humor. Often, the mental or physical aspects and features attracting him to a woman are the same that entertain him joyously and irreverently, suggest excessively exhilarating images to him, and encourage that pungent critical awareness, which in a very unusual way enriches rather than reduces his basic feeling for that woman. This total participation by Fellini — whether as a man or as a showman — occurs in all his relationships, not just to women, but to life and to other people in general. Who can say whether that participation is the cause or effect of his total lack of romanticism, of that mellow and virulent empathy with which he approaches people and objects, of that special and utterly tender "aesthetic displeasure" which in him seems to be the safest and most effective vehicle for penetrating the opaque denseness of reality.

The truth of the matter is that in Fellini's female universe — which he always feels as something "sweet and confused" — it is hard to tell what derives from a false and unrealistic upbringing and what is the unusual and fantastic legacy of the artist: that fluctuating unreality and that intense rarefaction that are typical of dream activity and that have even more agitated daily rhythms in Fellini.

To conclude, a both drastic and subjective theory: A man who lives so completely identified with his own work must necessarily have a rather peripheral and marginal private life, or else his private life is quickly transmuted in his tireless creative laboratory. Fellini has always struck me as a splendid instrument having extremely sensitive antennae that register everything around him, and as an extraordinary data-processing machine that translates and expresses whatever the antennae have gathered. Anything personal happening to the instrument probably concerns only its well-being and efficiency.

11

Giulietta

THE UTTERLY INDISPENSABLE person, the female presence that appears to ensure the splendid instrument's permanent cohesion, is Giulietta Masina.

Petite as she is, Giulietta has a bizarre temperament, whose contradictory and dynamic alchemy suggests the endless rippling of water, its infinite refraction. She is extroverted, vivacious, melancholy, sensitive, thoughtful and euphoric, sensible and unpredictable, sentimental and comical. The element amalgamating these often contrasting features is a curious, imperceptible absence, the slightest shadow of a trance. Giulietta has always reminded me of another person closely linked to Fellini: Nino Rota, who has composed the music for all his films. When I found out that music would have been the most authentic vocation for Giulietta too, my association struck me as less irrational. Furthermore, Fellini has a vaguely similar attitude when dealing with his wife and with his friend: the same way of being protective and solicitous, which, however, betrays a mysterious dependency.

Fellini and Giulietta have been married for over thirty years. Giulietta has both inspired and performed in several of Fellini's movies and is certainly a part, even if secret and indirect, of all the others.

The characters that Giulietta embodies in *La Strada, The Nights of Cabiria,* and *Juliet of the Spirits* clearly and painfully represent Fellini's complex and neurotic way of relating to women, like all Italian men of his generation. The premise of this irremediable shortcoming is usually: an adolescence dominated by the family, poisoned by a false and abstract education, distorted by ridiculous patriotic myths. And during that exciting but intoxicated period of psychological turmoil — the knowledge of women, of sex, a knowledge likewise constrained and divided into experiences that were mutilating because they were incompatible: brothels and matrimony. Cabiria, Juliet of the Spirits, but above all Gelsomina are female archetypes that denounce the profound mortification of women as sacrificial objects, as perennial victims. And those personages are also self-absolving projections of the male desire for a new innocence, a more rigorous internal cleanliness, a more adult spiritual morality. However, the basic irreparable impotence behind the projection is the same one condemning it to remain a projection. Hence, this ever frustrated striving can only be followed by a heavier sense of guilt and, thus, even more aggressive indemnities and outrages in a seesawing of contradictions that grow more and more lacerating and insoluble.

Giulietta is a sensitive and diligent actress, obedient and always open to Fellini's suggestions. Strangely, their few collisions, for instance on the set of *Juliet of the Spirits,* remind me — more than the usual ones between an actress and a director — of the subterranean skirmishes between a character and an author. And in this case, the skirmishes came close to their roles of husband and wife: for instance, Giulietta insisted on accentuating certain dramatic and emotional notes in her charac-

iulietta Masina in *The Nights of Cabiria*

Anthony Quinn as Zampanò in *La Strada*

Giulietta Masina as Gelsomina in *La Strada*

Giulietta Masina and Richard Basehart (il Matto) in *La Strada*

Giulietta Masina in *Juliet of the Spirits*

ellini at the filming of *Juliet of the Spirits*

Giulietta Masina visits Fellini during the filming of 8½

ter, whereas Fellini disagreed, impatient, quarrelsome, and thus already in the wrong.

Fellini's relationship to Giulietta is made up of the private and simple daily habits of indisputable unions, the kind that make the reasons for staying together more inexplicable, yet more important than any obvious and secondary reasons for splitting up. Such relations may have exhausted their dynamic substance without being themselves exhausted. After a risky transition, they can become irreplaceable structures that each partner takes over from the other; they can respond to needs that will not be suppressed or satisfied; they can evolve into an at times difficult discipline that often permits fulfilling a destiny. For an essentially voracious and eccentric nature like Fellini's, Giulietta is the solid nucleus, the axle guaranteeing its integrity.

Once, Giulietta showed up during the filming of *Satyricon*. Giulietta almost never visits a Fellini set, though she remains in steady contact with it because the director keeps telephoning her all the time: brief calls, rapid greetings, telegraphic recommendations and requests that mask the need to feel a presence, to know Giulietta is there.

The day of her visit, we were preparing to shoot one of the most terrifying sequences in *Satyricon*, the collapse of the Insula Felicles. For scenes like this, there can be only one take. So the atmosphere in the studio was overheated with suspense, curiosity, fear, turmoil. Giulietta discreetly murmured hello, then sat down in a corner, took some pink yarn out of her bag, and started knitting away, tranquil and attentive to what was happening around her. The workmen were all in their places, ready to remove the wooden beams buttressing the various parts of the Insula that were supposed to shatter on the ground. The silence was spasmodic, but tinged with an amused cynicism — people always expect things to go wrong. All you could hear was the humming of the camera.

Then Fellini began shouting the numbers of the various sections that were to plunge down sequentially. "One! . . . Two! . . ." The silence was as undisturbed as the immobility of the edifice. The Insula tenants scurried around, but their panic made no sense in that serene tranquillity. "Three! . . .

Four! . . ." A pair of rocks rolled lazily and indecisively toward the ground. "Five! . . . Six! . . ." The Insula was still upright, inexplicably solid. The two blocks of polystyrene had been removed at certain points, and those were the only places where you could see the paper wall. Stagehands, looking like enormous reeling rats, frantically pushed away at the paper wall with beams or tore through it by knocking down the props. You expected the Count of Monte Cristo to emerge at any moment.

Without missing a stitch, Giulietta curiously and uncertainly watched what was happening.

At the third try, the Insula gave way and collapsed in a maelstrom of dust and rocks. The extras — half-naked, howling men, women, and children — scurried like maddened lizards from their nests. Their horror was still unjustified but at least lifelike in that storm of papier-mâché. The horses, terrified by the din, the dust, the bouncing rocks, incapable of seeing through the sham, leaped from the stalls, crashed to the ground, threw themselves into the small courtyard pool, scrambled wildly to get out, galloped madly toward the camera. At times like these, Fellini normally vanishes, dissolves into thin air. There are endless anecdotes about how uncontrollably impressionable he is with horses, to whose skittishness he responds with his very own skittishness. (In fact, there's one story, which, if it's made up, then is so purely by chance. One day, a producer offered Fellini a blank check to make a Western. After conferences and negotiations, the agreement was just about to be reached when Fellini casually remarked: "It's understood, of course, that the only horses in the movie will be rocking horses. . . ." The project collapsed.)

Yet in the dust swirled up by the Insula earthquake, amid the dreadful screams of the victims, no one could help noticing, incredulously, that this time Fellini remained by the camera to the very end, calm, even ostentatiously imperturbable, while nearly everybody else was scrambling higgledy-piggledy toward the back of the studio, pursued by furious galloping horses with steaming nostrils.

That same instant, Giulietta, quietly amused, went back to her knitting after looking up for a split second.

This episode contains perhaps the most accurate image of their relationship. If Giulietta is nearby, she gives Fellini a greater self-assurance in tackling, and abandoning himself more freely to, his own disquieting visions.

12

The Insane Asylum

"You wanna come along to the insane asylum? The head of the Psychiatric Hospital of Monte Mario has given us permission to visit the place. After a consultation, we can decide whether or not to leave you there!" Fellini's voice on the phone was cheerful and joking. I said yes without quite understanding what it was all about.

We arrived at the Provincial Hospital of Santa Maria della Pietà: a name less allusive than intimidating in its bureaucratic precision. Fellini had the vivid impatience, the fervid and delicate attentiveness of a bloodhound hot on a trail. To me, there was something unnerving in the hospital's name. Contrary to habit, Fellini preferred using his own solid Mercedes instead of my old Fiat. The choice was probably random, but it struck me as a security measure, a defense.

The insane asylum is made up of some twenty pavilions scat-

tered through a park. The pavilions are old and seem abandoned and poor, like certain sanatoriums in the country. The
park is immense and well cared for, but it doesn't take much to
realize that this care is nothing but a sort of vegetable anemia,
the orderliness of penury, the singular neatness of a very slow
abstention. The hospital altogether has the dismal immutability
of places that house a human condition without altering it, just
passively gathering its time, like orphan asylums or old-age
homes.

Here too, as elsewhere, one feels an atmosphere of respite,
the inactivity of a Saturday afternoon. The paths are deserted
and silent, and it's all a bit chilling. It gave our visit a more
direct and hazardous intimacy.

Our Virgil was a psychiatrist of the hospital, a young man
with a dark, soft face. He didn't have the secure and protective
look of an official guide, but seemed more like those guides with
an exact knowledge of the places to visit, who, because of that
knowledge, are scared and try to mix in with the group they are
guiding, demanding its support and solidarity. Our strange and
simpatico Virgil asked Fellini which pavilion he wanted to visit
first. Fellini, for an instant, had the voracious and frowning uncertainty of a man who refuses to forgo anything. Meanwhile,
we got into the car. The Mercedes had only two doors, and
climbing in was a laborious maneuver.

We began with the pavilion for working women. The door
was opened by a very fat, very rosy nun. Our arrival seemed almost to pull her out of her occupation without disturbing her;
she would easily return to it when we were gone. Like all the
nuns in charge of the various pavilions, there was something
meek about her, absentminded, almost mortified.

The "working women" are destined, at least theoretically, to
remain locked up until the very end of their days. Perhaps
that's why their pavilion has the definitive and almost comforting peace of a convent. Furthermore, the work these women
do — sewing, darning, laundry, ironing — gives them a pre-
tense of archaic, familiar humanity, the illusion of an exchange,
of a relationship with the outside, even if the concrete expression of that relationship is fatefully destroyed by the magic cir-

cle of their insanity. In fact, no sooner did we enter a workroom with five women bent over enormous black sewing-machines than they brusquely stopped working and looked up at us. They were rigid, motionless, their eyes direct and impenetrable through entangled hair. They seemed like five quiet animals raising their heads for one instant from their feed.

Fellini dragged along affectionately behind Agnesina, a girl with a pear-shaped head and a huge nose. Blushing to be the center of so much interest, she kept giggling and holding one hand in front of her mouth to hide her emotions. She had the docile and emaciated look of the eternal lay-sister and maid-of-all-work.

Today was Shrove Saturday, and the women were fervently and festively kneading and baking the traditional carnival tarts. An enormous, big-boned woman with an innocent, flour-covered face offered us a tart. Fellini took a bite, but held the rest of the tart in his hand with childlike indecisiveness until he reached the next pavilion. I took two tarts. They were obviously tarts and they were even excellent, but I gulped them down with an anxious, exaggerated goodwill, as if they were something different, something inedible.

The "criminal" pavilion houses the famous L.A., who committed two murders and attempted a third one. He remains aloof, discreet, almost distinguished notwithstanding the pajamas. His eyes are keen and cruel, a splendid black mustachio gives him the easygoing and disheveled look of a sculptor. When Fellini asked him about the reasons for and length of his stay here, he replied promptly and politely, raising his arms and bowing impeccably, like a person trying to avoid an issue. "Ah, I really wouldn't know, I simply don't know." As if the matter concerned someone else, and the man with the large mustache wanted that humble and solemn tone to dissipate Fellini's impolite curiosity without disappointing it.

A boy of eighteen, an ex-sailor from La Spezia, was sprawling on a couch. He was raving away, feverishly repeating: "They all know I was kicked out, they all know I was kicked out . . ." The schizophrenic delirium seems to create a real magnetic field. Any person or object entering that physical space was instantly magnetized and integrated in the delirium. In fact, Fellini only had to take a step toward the boy for him to ask: "Are you an admiral? Then you know, they all know that I was kicked out. . . ." Fellini, as always when in direct contact with a sick man, was deeply moved, almost suffering, and he candidly corrected him, saying he was only a friend of the doctor's.

Next, he found himself in front of a person about whom he later would frequently speak with an amused and distressed nostalgia. This meeting, with its decidedly humorous and grotesque touches, would remain oddly comforting and meaningful in his memory. The man had been in bed for several days because of bad feet. For thirty years, he had been pulling the cart of dirty laundry down the lanes of the park, from pavilion to pavilion, as unflinching and indefatigable as a beast of burden. A job practiced so long and so generously by a man with an elementary or inert mind ultimately had to change him physically. Indeed, the man looked like a donkey, he had a long face, an equine grin, and two huge flapping ears from which you could almost see a feedbag hanging. The conversation that followed between the man and the nurse, then with Fellini, was a tiny jewel of applied Zen. In the space of a very brief, and perturbingly and astonishingly simple dialogue, any traditional idea of feeling and custom was crushed and shattered. The only thing left intact was *Being*, in all its mystery, intolerant of any definition. He was asked: How old are you? Are your parents living? How long have you been here? Do you like it here? And each time, the ineffable donkey fired back: "Well? Well? Well?" Then he bowed his head to the side, raised his eyebrows, and yielded to an alarming grin of indulgence. The discomfort, the confusion, the slight embarrassment provoked by this string of impatient and unanswerable *well*s were the exact equivalent of all the comical futility that he dared to defy. Our friend's spherical wisdom halted for only an instant, showing the passionate imperfection of feeling, when he was asked: "Where is Poldo?" He replied, calm and serious: "Poldo is dead." Who was Poldo? Perhaps a real donkey, who was his work companion for a long time.

At close inspection, just what is the profound wisdom of those *wells*? He no longer seemed so much like a donkey. The ocher color of his face, the close-cropped jet-black hair could be those of an ancient Mediterranean philosopher or a Carthaginian sage.

We were confused as we left him, while the exterior amusement of the episode gradually turned into an intimate, beneficent sensation of peace and well-being.

A sensation, however, which had to be set aside momentarily. We were ushered into the vast hall of the epileptics with its ever-heavy atmosphere of a brewing tempest. An ancient, respectable gentleman in drawers was standing by the window, conversing animatedly with an invisible interlocutor. A robust fellow cheerfully greeted us in a booming voice; his wrists were firmly bound to the sides of his bed. He roared that he wanted to tell Fellini his fiancée's name, but very privately. Fellini bent his ear to that noisy crater. He was a bit scared and hesitant as if the obstreperous youth might bite it off at any moment. The fiancée's name was Anna Zanotti.

In the women's pavilions, the madness seemed, at first sight, to be weakened by female passivity and frivolity. But we quickly realized that these attributes made the misery even more ignoble. A country squiress regally leaning on a bunch of pillows, her arms crossed over her chest, stared at us most serenely and fixedly as though we were objects for her eyes to rest on. She had a round head swathed in tresses, and her eyes were blue. Our greetings left her quite indifferent. But upon moving away, we heard a placid, cartoonlike *"Ciao."* Another little old lady with a meek look and white hair was having vegetable soup; her gusto was incredible, it was sheer reverence. She answered Fellini's question with an overly mincing and blissful smile, like a dreadful witch intent on beguiling a child: "Oh this soup is *so* good. If I didn't have some every evening, I couldn't sleep a wink."

Deliriums, soliloquys, obstinate or forgetful silences in each bed.

From behind one door, an unbelievably powerful tenor exploded into "La Donna è Mobile." He sang the whole aria and then repeated it. This solo was deafening, but the nurses and visitors continued whatever they were doing, undisturbed, as though not hearing anything. I felt ill at ease.

I caught sight of Fellini at the end of a corridor. His face was slightly reddened, his eyes were big, he was agitated, vulnerable, he seemed to be in a fascinating and busy state of alarm. Next to him was the head of the hospital, a wiry little man with a long geometrical face, a horselike smile, often dreamy, as if suggesting or inviting, and a short, gray, very distinguished beard. His eyes were green, perpetually trying to investigate or be patient, with something possessed about them, a restrained and slightly transfixed liveliness. He was listening to "the girl sheriff," a lovely twenty-year-old with a fine, pallid face and long black hair falling on her shoulders. Her light hazel eyes had the cruel and impassive fixity of birds; her lips were dry and cracked. She had on a nylon housecoat with a floral pattern.

We were made ill at ease by her way of absolutely and unabashedly ignoring the people listening curiously to her. She talked only to the doctor. She spoke about gunfights, sheriffs, about Dallas, where she works as a sheriff, about Kennedy's assassination, about squalid rooming houses near the railroad station where a gynecologist forced her to do a striptease and a friend of his raped her. She used a lot of English words with the free-and-easy approximation of the uneducated. Her verbal delirium had the aggressive and sarcastic plausibility of certain prostitutes in a police station. "I know that Fellini's come to the hospital. . . . But where is he? . . ." Fellini was introduced to her and now he had the insecure and embarrassed air of someone acting a role. The "girl sheriff" took leave, arrogantly demanding a part in one of his films, but then, with a smile of condescension and haughty indulgence for those present, she quickly added: "But I can only do the part of Ringo!"

We went back to the men's pavilions. A little monster some twenty inches high was being walked through the corridors in full display, like an adorable mascot.

In an incredibly smelly cell, an old gentleman, buried under the covers and engulfed in his own excrement as in a placenta, murmured to Fellini that he was indeed feeling a bit better.

A southern boy came over to Fellini. He had the big face of a
sleepy and voracious kid, and an unmotivated ecstatic smile that
never stopped throughout the conversation. He stared at Fellini
as though he were a marvelous toy and he paid him compliments as though they were the official and incontrovertible ut-
terance of a medical diagnosis: "You are the famous director
Fellini? It is a great honor to meet you. You are a great director, you know? A terrific director. I have seen all your films.
You're a damn fine director! Terrific!" Under this barrage of admiration, Fellini burst out laughing, then drew back, still smiling, intimidated and ill at ease, as if all such enthusiasm in this
place were a colossal and somewhat insolent joke. The boy's
name was Peppino. Fellini interrupted him, asking why he was
in the hospital. Peppino, without lessening his big smile of
amazed excitement, told him: "I had a major nervous break-
down. I was arrested by the police in my town because I kept
going to graveyards with my transistor radio turned on full
blast. I had the idea of resurrecting the dead that way."

In the pavilion of the insane, the most desperate sight is that
of the young. Their vitality is consumed in senseless mechanical
actions, in exhausting and inextinguishable tics. Faces of carnival masks or of wrinkled crones, grimaces, continuous rhythmic movements of the limbs or head, naked backs and poste-
riors emerging and vanishing under white gowns. A dear little
woman, slender and modest looking, was literally pecking at
biscuits like a hen. Her baby was sprawled on her bed, its arms
open and abandoned, its mouth full of a yellowish mash, while a
transistor radio blared at full volume on its belly. The mother
was feeding her little boy, tenderly raising his head. She turned
to Fellini as though to ask for an explanation, a bit of advice,
some precaution to follow: "He's not speaking now, he doesn't
say a word, all he likes is songs."

That mother and son seemed like the integral, almost blasphemous version of the *Pietà*. The picture was brutally realistic,
a heartrending and innocent realism that was far more abstract
and effective than any artistic speculation. That is the only way
to explain why the agitation and sorrow were not totally overwhelming. For the first and only time, I saw Fellini hurry away

with moist eyes. By trying to contain my feelings, I ended up with an unbearable headache.

Now the visit was concluded. We stepped into the director's office. A huge lithograph of a madman's drawing hung on the wall. It was a striking vast choral construction of writhing naked bodies.

Fellini tried to explain to the doctor why he had come to the hospital. His words in the context of diffidence, reticence, and guilt, separating the madman and his milieu from the rest of the world, sounded like a timid justification. Fellini was still a bit upset. His eyes glowed and his face was ruddy, like someone who's been close to fire for a long time. His voice had become even thinner, softer, at times slightly tremulous:

"My reason for coming here is not directly linked to the film I am now preparing, it has no documentary or informational significance. That is to say, my film is not about madmen or insane asylums. I am visiting these places simply in quest of emotions, suggestions that can then be translated into something else, into exact psychological and environmental solutions for the story I intend to tell. The main character of the film will be going through a total alienation from himself and everything around him. For this, madness can be an effective and stimulating analogy."

The doctor nodded his head, satisfied but inexpressive. He accompanied us to the barred gate and took leave with a tranquil smile.

As we drove back to town, Fellini was euphoric and talkative. He recalled his visit to the insane asylum of Magliano with Mario Tobino prior to filming *The Nights of Cabiria*. It had been a kind of citadel forgotten by God and men. In his memory, the Magliano experience had become a sort of grandiose and terrifying epic of madness.

He spoke about the hospital, the nurses, the head physician, the people he had met, with an excited, liberating rage, revealing his humanity as a conscious sympathy.

"Did you see those eyes? Even the eyes of those who weren't so seriously ill, the more normal ones? They have something 'different' about them, an enigmatic expressiveness of another species. Madness is imprisoning, but why couldn't it also be a higher degree of freedom? A madman no longer has emotional ties, he's released from any conceptual, ethical, social system, he so totally identifies with his delirium, he becomes his delirium, and in this so perfect adherence to his own state, this inevitable and gratuitous adherence, he achieves his own freedom."

I objected that that could be so when seen from the outside by him, Federico Fellini, a sane man, or rather a prisoner of real demands and conceptual categories. If a madman is no longer subject to any sort of conceptualization, then any presumed concept of freedom has neither validity nor meaning. "Well of course as seen by me, and by whom else?" replied Fellini. My objection was rather obvious. I went on undaunted, saying that otherwise even a rock is completely itself, hence free, but this type of liberty also contains the notion of regression.

Fellini won't tolerate being trapped in any all-too-rigorous and mechanical dialectical skirmishes (a healthy intolerance, since formal thought and a logical schema do not explain reality, they introduce slogans to tame it for collective use). So at this point he started joking: "As a matter of fact, I've known rocks with an ineffable expression of happiness and freedom! . . . I meant that a rock is completely free in the sense that it realizes itself in being simply an assemblage of atoms all forming a lump of matter. And besides, who can say why those places never make me sad, never depress me. On the contrary, they seem comforting, protective."

Perhaps, I suggested, it was the tranquillity, that serene silence of one's own fear in extreme situations. All the more so when concerning other people.

"It's not precisely that. Ordinarily, people see life as a horizontal line made of order, sense, consistency, all in all something rather unrealistic and wretched," Fellini went on in that slightly joking tone that seems to belie his words. "The presence of madness and its infinite aspects, the presence of holiness or genius, shatters that horizontal line and transforms it into an unclassifiable zigzag, something inexplicable, at times no longer referrable, but containing the most authentic, the most profound meaning of life. That's why when I go to find madmen, I feel serene and hopeful. Because theirs is above all a testimony to disorder and darkening, but at the same time the prodigious and reassuring confirmation that order, harmony, knowledge are not necessarily the turf of those who aren't mad. Since my childhood, I've always been fascinated by that kind of abnormalcy. When I was playing in the courtyard, I would sometimes suddenly see the enormous dangling head of the mongoloid boy on the fourth floor of our building. I would stop playing and just stare up, spellbound, until that head vanished."

Fellini kept talking in an absorbed and solitary eagerness, as though, instead of speaking, he were writing to clarify and keep intact the emotion and meaning of what he had seen. I felt as if I had a troublesome fever preventing my usual contact with my surroundings. Every so often, I brought up some episode or other, but only to neutralize it, talking about it so that the specter would not haunt me obsessively. Fellini left, kissing me and smirking "Well? Well? Well?" to ease my confusion.

13

I Don't Know You ... Who Are You?

THE NOTES FELLINI makes to register gradually certain details or elements of a film are as suggestive, ambiguous, and indecipherable as any jottings in the world.

Here is a series of notes from the journal on *G. Mastorna*. The first page has a conspicuous maxim in red:

> "The most sacred thing is the thing you are dealing with at the moment."

> IMPORTANT: Provide information on the consciousness and the ego to the figures of the unconscious (or the spirits of the dead, who are the same thing). Hence, a correct intuition — the old idea of having the airline hostess ask G. Mastorna for news about life on earth.

ellini filming *Satyricon*

Fanfulla (Vernacchio) and Max Born (Gitone) in *Satyricon*

Vernacchio, drawn by Fellini

ellini on the set of *Satyricon*

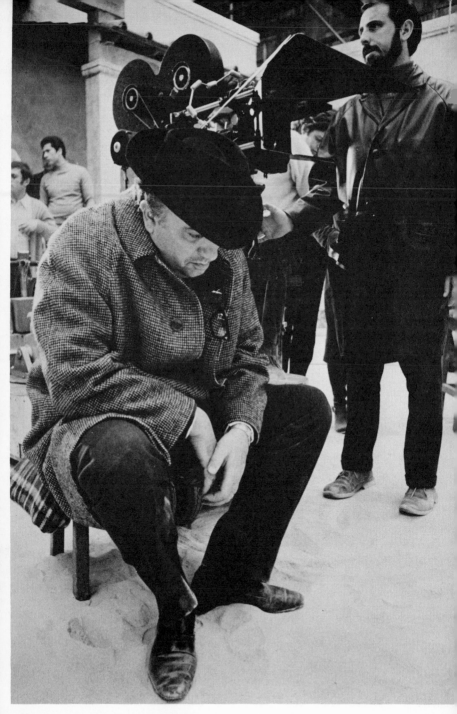

A break during the filming of *Satyricon*

SOUL (Hostess): Scoffing, ironical, seductive, mendacious, unfaithful.

To SPEAK with one's own SOUL. WRITE letters to it. It WILL ANSWER.

IDEAS — NOTES
1) And what if they make him up in the car (a huge, old Cadillac) while driving him (Mastorna) to the Oscar ceremony? The car also contains the make-up mirror with all the lightbulbs in its frame.
2) VALDEMARO (old vaudeville comic) for the wizard.
3) *TV screen.* In the huge Neapolitan room.
4) While stretched out on the bed and watching the TV, from which the clown smiles at him, Mastorna falls asleep. The phone jangles. Dialogue with the *unknown friend,* closed eyes, never lifting the receiver, and almost totally in long shot. Then close-up of awakening; the porter is already in the room.
5) The mistress could be the owner of a grocery store?
6) Armandino appears as "that Neapolitan figure" who does publicity for the stores?

The following notes, often illustrated with sketches and colored drawings, were made for *Satyricon:*

SATYRICON
(There are different vibrations in the air)

	INCANDESCENCE
Science-fiction	harsh
Madness	barbaric
Martians	hallucinatory
Nazis	neurotic
	psychedelic

EVERYTHING is already in the frescoes.

Dusty fragments. As though trying to reconstruct a very ancient amphora from the shards found after centuries.

Dust and darkness. Evocation by a medium. Stopping in briefer and briefer passages: ". . . And the old man laughed, pointing his crooked finger at something that the others had not yet noticed."

"The horse bathed in sweat. . . ."

". . . The sun setting behind the villa. . . ."

". . . The eyes were melancholy. . . ."

And darkness, long black tails. . . . Silence. . . . A voice still saying something, silence. . . . The closing credits.

BAS-RELIEFS — Dreadful   fixity — smiles   and gazes of wild animals.

The festivals: the night was ablaze with fireworks, huge bonfires everywhere in town and country.

Theater — the actor's stand-in was often a criminal who was actually executed on stage for the sake of the narrative.

Collapse of the houses.

The skyscraper.

Crazy proportions and disproportions in both the architecture, the statues, and even the film images, with tiny and gigantic men. The huge head of the Colossus hauled on an enormous cart, making the houses collapse.

IMPORTANT: Make up the dogs. Unknown breeds of animals.

IMPORTANT: gestures, winks, grimaces never seen accompany the dialogues.

It's like being inside the *sun*. It's an incandescent dimension, anyone living in it has different eyes, different nervous rhythms . . . (don't forget the dream of the rosy madmen who were in this over-heated, quivering dimension).

INCANDESCENT MADNESS
I DON'T KNOW YOU
WHO ARE YOU?

IMPORTANT: arrhythmia, scrawny, askew. BADLY PLAYED. As though the actors were performing poorly. Fixed stares or feverishly wandering eyes, prolonged silences, something brittle, hesitant, stammering in speech. . . .
Trifena has a caged slave in her hold, he has to comb her *because she's bald.*
The statues of Venus and Mars that unite because of the magnet inside. Mina or Quartilla? Or Tri-fena? She sings with the imprisoned Beatles!?!

TRIMALCHIO: during the visit to Trimalchio's sta-bles a demonstration of his horse: marble stable, ivory trough covered with purple; gem-studded horse-collars.

Always think of the demonstrations of the gladia-tors in the streets.
At Trimalchio's banquet, he gets up every so often and goes and screws. (Remember Caligula, who would go off with the wives of his guests and, upon returning after having them, he would praise their talents or loudly disparage their de-fects. A husband who protested was killed at the table. Also remember the guy who pretended to sleep rather than see his wife kissed and felt up by Trimalchio. They dry their hands on the heads of slaves and the breasts of slave-girls.)
One of Trimalchio's concubines has a white head

and a red forehead: "You look like snow stained by wine." Triangular privies for vomiting.

Greater stress during the film on consulting oracles and drawing omens from anything: the flight of birds.

14

The Ship of Jules Verne

At this point, Fellini's personal and very private relationship to the film is enriched by new media; it is made more precise and amplified by the first collaborators: the possible co-authors of the treatment and the script.

The indispensable condition for a rapport between Fellini and his collaborators is a common language, an identical system of psychological, emotional, or intellectual relationships.

The understanding is established by certain typical expressions, daily terms: Fellini's torrential, eclectic, fascinating chats, in which he indicates what he has in mind, the intentions and objectives of the film, with a dense network of examples, metaphors, similes, suggestions, paradoxes, hypotheses, and syntheses. Some of them decidedly unique and hence all the more effective.

Obviously, such a torrent of excitement must find a proper

soil in the other person, a congenial receptiveness, so as to achieve some meaning and become constructive. Suppose Fellini, in trying to explain a certain ambience, compared it to the particular atmosphere of Piazza Indipendenza at three on a Sunday afternoon in July. It would be disastrously funny if he were asked: "Why? What happens on Piazza Indipendenza at three on a Sunday afternoon?"

Describing the work habits, the concrete occasions when the subject and script of a Fellini film are born and develop, would require a phantomlike, often untraceable itinerary. And the *least* that could happen would be to lose the trail.

Under these circumstances, the only people who could give a true account of the route would be Fellini's first travel companions: the scriptwriters.

"Doing a script for Fellini," says Bernardino Zapponi, "is like sailing on a Jules Verne ship in quest of uncharted seas. Incredible panoramas and personages waft by on the horizon. In order to get a better look, Fellini pulls back his head, opens his eyes wide, and hums or whistles. We tell one another about the things we've seen. We chat for whole afternoons, abandoning ourselves to the childlike joy of inventing stories. We make absurd suggestions, we find undreamed-of connections. Eventually, Fellini 'settles the account.' He has a mathematical sense of order, a love of numbers, which, incidentally, shows in his pet habit of making actors count instead of talk. He is excellent in drawing out the exact figures, the strict data of a problem. Like every truly imaginative author, he is guided by a precise and unfathomable sense of inevitable geometrical laws.

"Apparently distracted, inattentive, absentminded, Fellini as a scriptwriter stimulates, provokes, retorts, listens to the echo of his own restless drumming. He tries various ways, even concretely. Often, the script conferences take place in a car, his skidding auto, that seems to obey his changing moods: it speeds up, slows down, groans in its choked engine, turns into dark streets. Even in cheerful and rambling conversations, he is given no peace by his obsession of an author doomed to a constructive system. He feels compelled to systematize, he has a need to pigeonhole every idea that can become an image.

"When I think of Fellini, I never see the face that normally appears in newspapers, the cordial, youthful, cheerfully tender man. Instead, I see the restless, painful, even somber expression of a man withdrawn into evasive solitude. He can free himself from his torments only with a continuously nurtured faith in imagination and creation. For instance, when we were working on the story of *Toby Dammit*, which was remotely inspired by a tale of Poe's, we wandered through deserted *trattorias* and luncheonettes on the outskirts of town. And especially, we strolled along the boardwalk of Ostia, the ravaged and desolate beach — as fascinating in its winter abandonment as a city after an atomic explosion. Such hopelessness gave birth to the story of a mad, drug-addicted actor who comes to die in Rome. Fellini loves squalor. In reality, squalor is tragic and poetic. An empty restaurant, or untenanted ramshackle hotel in Fascist style, has the magic of things beyond time, beyond history, things that were never born and hence can never die. Squalor never ages. It is something that has taken a wrong turn, winding up and remaining on a dead track.

"Working with Fellini does not tire us, despite the necessary creative effort. The absence of real fatigue is due to the total liberty of inspiration, of unbridled amusement in telling stories. Fellini leads his collaborators into a rarefied, magical atmosphere, which we hate to leave."

Thus the script for a Fellini film is the both exact and ambiguous route of the film from its author to its realization. Hence, the script can be only an allusive echo of the film. The mood, the meaning, the quivering vitality of the film must necessarily become hazy and pallid in the precision of literary detail. At certain points, Fellini may even consider the script somehow inadequate or alien, like describing a painting with a cybernetic formula or musical notes. The script may weigh upon him with an inevitable force, he fears it as though it could imprison or distract him, as though he were caught in litigious and guilt-ridden confrontations. But all that is probably a simple precaution of the film's instinct to avoid any long halt in its own development. In fact, a Fellini script does not really translate the danger of too much creative liberty into a constructive dis-

The director kneels down to the producer. Marcello Mastroianni as Guido in 8½

cipline. The script is actually a factor of basic and irreplaceable clarification of the film.

Fellini is particularly stubborn in having the readers of his scripts base their opinions exclusively on what they read rather than on being influenced or enriched by any hypothetical filming that the figure of the director might suggest. An affectionate solidarity is always aroused by his insecurity, his malaise in waiting for judgments. And one can only admire his critical intelligence in deflating ill-founded negative responses, his equanimity in accepting stupidly exaggerated ones, the thoughtfulness he saves for the truly appropriate verdicts.

A Fellini script can provoke the most unbelievable reactions and misunderstandings. Thus, a man of good sense doggedly focused on an epigram by Stirner that happened to occur in the *Mastorna* script. The man, on the wrong track, saw the script as

Screening the tests. Guido Albert as Pace the producer in 8½

Fellini with Angelo Rizzolo, the producer of 8½

a kind of cinematic testimony to that philosopher's nihilism. The producer De Laurentiis, on the other hand, is a superstitious Neapolitan. He attended the conference after the script reading, and whenever they discussed the subject, the odyssey of a dead man, De Laurentiis would frantically touch an unmentionable part of his body, which is supposed to ward off evil spirits.

A famous writer called the movie project "highly ambitious." Fellini, genuinely surprised, answered: "What does *ambitious* mean? Ambition is a crucial psychological mainspring for an artist. It's like telling an expectant woman: 'You know, you're too pregnant.' "

15

The Vice-President's Underpants

WHILE STILL WORKING on one movie, Fellini is nearly always thinking of the next. And to that extent, everything goes very well. He also seems absolutely incapable of thinking about a film if he doesn't have a signed contract with a producer. It's as though the film acquires some mysterious necessity from a concrete production relationship. And yet this remains within the limits of a perhaps bizarre discipline, even though it often turns out to be risky, since the first producer of a Fellini film is rarely the one who finally does produce the film.

The efforts, the complications begin for Fellini with the hunt for financiers, for money. For some time now, the capital has been coming almost exclusively from large American companies, and the Americans have two very distinct and very incompatible reactions to a director like Fellini: a highly vivid interest and a highly vivid distrust (a businessman's snobbery and

greedy materialism). Moreover, the Italian producer of the film
may belong to either of two professional categories: he may
have the free and easy manner of a rogue or the passivity and
lack of initiative of a bank teller.

Under these circumstances, if Fellini wants to make the
movie, he is often forced to intervene directly in the preliminary work, take an active part in the negotiations, be present at
the meetings and conferences with the backers — in a word,
become something like his own producer.

The prototype of such preliminary discussions — and this is
no exaggeration — can look something like this: A vast suite in
the Grand Hotel; at a table in a vast room, the Italian producer, Fellini, and the host: the American representative, with
a cigar wedged in his mouth and the slightly sinister air that important people always have when their physical looks are insignificant. Attempts are made to start a conversation. After the
first five sentences, the telephone jangles. It is on the table,
next to a bottle of mineral water and some glasses. Los Angeles
or New York on the line. For three-quarters of an hour, at the
constant risk of going deaf forever and with the obvious effect of
making his guests lose their patience, the American bawls and
sniggers into the phone as though he were in a desert with the
life-and-death problem of getting someone to hear him. Then
he hangs up. Further attempts are made to resume the dialogue. But after another five sentences, the American excuses
himself, gets up, and locks himself into the bathroom. The
others hear running water, splashes. An elementary deductive
reasoning can only conclude that the vice-president of the big
American production company is indulging in a bidet wash or
even a bath. The reasons for choosing such an untimely occasion
to absent himself for these personal attentions seem anything
but elementary. They hint at inscrutable necessities, at refined
and mysterious habits.

The vice-president reappears after half an hour, with new
vigor and in his shorts. As can happen in a contact with madness, the Yankee's naturalness and courteous nonchalance in
ignoring his unusual semiattire make Fellini and the Italian producer feel out of place and ill at ease, even though they are fully

...lini with Giulietta Masina, Dino De Laurentiis (standing, far left), and Tullio Pinelli ...tting, far left) at the Oscar awards for *Cabiria*, Hollywood 1957

and impeccably dressed. The American's sudden whim greatly amuses Fellini, rearousing his interest in the negotiations, which now move along properly, alternating only with the American's rapid and excusable exits to the bedroom. Then the telephone jangles again. This time, it's Istanbul. A mere fifteen minutes of a delirious monologue by a bushman lost in the jungle. Now it's Fellini's turn. He grabs the telephone and settles deep into an armchair.

The vice-president in underpants seizes the opportunity to whisper something to the Italian producer with the good sense of the buyer asking for legitimate information on the temperament of a horse that he intends to purchase: "Is it true that Fellini has put off *Mastorna* and wants to make *Satyricon* because a witch predicted he would have two failures after *Juliet of the Spirits* — in this case, the Poe episode and *Satyricon* itself?" This question is far more serious than the ablutions or the freakiness of the underpants. A regressive abyss yawns, and an adult business meeting drops to the level of kindergarten curiosity. The Italian, either in secret complicity or else truly stunned and disarmed by his colleague's unbelievable question, retorts with an equally serious and placid negation: "It's not true." And in a suddenly heavier Neapolitan accent, he promptly adds a eulogy — so laconic and absurd in its banality that it sounds deadly — "Fellini is an indefatigable worker!"

The route to financing a Fellini film is so torturous, so thick with tensions and anxieties, that if the producer doesn't have robust nerves and a love of risk, he will suffer from depressions, dizziness, and endless troubles. One morning, Fellini was asked point-blank for the instant return of four hundred million lire, the entire mortgage on *Mastorna*. To which he simply and tranquilly replied: "It's like asking me for Piazza di Spagna. Come and get it."

In its ranks, the movie world also has a few ardent men of honor who explain this hysterical instability of producers, offering reasons that are so improbable as to be comical: "It's about time Fellini gave up his habit of calling his producer '*Ciccio bello*' [old boy]. If it were just Fellini, it might be bearable. But the deplorable fact is that in Fellini's wake, the other directors in the producer's stable all take the same disrespectful liberty. Luckily, once they're discouraged, they instantly stop and mend their ways. But Fellini stubbornly persists in his scandalous behavior." In other words: Either stop calling me "old boy" or else give me back my four hundred million lire.

The financial squalls and mishaps of a Fellini film stop only when the movie has been finished, never earlier, as though they were the economic equivalent of unforeseeable restless waverings or internal motions that accompany it to the very end. For instance, when *La Dolce Vita* was three-quarters done, it was still the object of frantic secret transactions between producers, as though it were stolen goods, contagious material, or a live bomb.

16

The Magic Circle

THE LEGAL ACT of signing the contract with the producer is
immediately followed by at least the concrete preparation of the
film.

Until it appears on the screen, a Fellini movie goes through a
steady, unforeseeable metamorphosis. The most magical and
crucial element of that metamorphosis is the preparation, during which the film passes from a temporary effervescence of
possibilities and experiments to its true shape.

A Fellini film emerges, grows, and affirms itself in a natural,
spontaneous, autonomous atmosphere. During the preparation,
these features become exaggerated: the stubborn efforts to cope
with the anything but natural demands of the production and,
paradoxically, to subordinate the very goal of finishing the
movie. Hence, it is not unusual, say, for the general organizer
of the film to lock himself up in the office with Fellini, just

three days before the start of shooting, in order to make him decide whether or not to leave out a certain sequence. Likewise, the art director, looking for all the world like a monstrous insect, laden with models, photos, blueprints, laboriously trudges behind Fellini, begging for an opinion, a suggestion, a sketch — something definite on the setting of a scene. Or else the assistant director, with skillful and anxious nonchalance, reminds him that he still has to — oh! it's certainly not urgent — select an actor for an important role that hasn't been cast yet.

Now if all those things are *not* exceptional, then Fellini's reactions *are*. Confronted with the firmness of the organizer, he tries to oppose it with impossible arguments that are meant to be practical and rational, or else he tells bare-faced lies. He demolishes the art director's insistence with a vague promise, an impassive, deadly silence, or with a grimace and a quip, expressing so much doubt that his co-worker is momentarily hypnotized or even utterly enraptured. As for the tactful zeal of the assistant director, Fellini rewards it by lowering the number of possible actors for the given character from fifteen to twelve.

The psychological demands are so compact and steady that the preparation for a Fellini film becomes a kind of exclusive spiritual retreat for all the participants. Fellini may wake up the art director 3 A.M. to explain the new figurative shape he intends to give to a situation. He throws the production manager out of bed at six on a Sunday morning and drags him off to Viterbo: he wants to shoot inside the fire station there. Will he be able to? He orders the assistant director into his office at two on an August afternoon: they have to pick the extras for the background of a scene that isn't scheduled for another six months. The setting may be anywhere: a school, a nightclub, a station, a hospital, a church. Fellini will recruit the actors by fishing them promiscuously from the most contrasting files: Dirty Faces, Attractive Gracile Girls, Comical Ingenues, Clowns, Sophisticated Melancholy Women, Robust Homosexuals, Male Hustlers. He makes an appointment with the almost-definitely-cast lead actor at eleven at night and drives him to Ostia in order to chat a bit, get to know him better, and initiate the actor/character association, whose formula has long been so mysterious and obscure for Fellini.

During the preparatory phase, the scriptwriters never stop orbiting around the film, for the scenes may be altered or rewritten until the very last takes. From the opposite direction, the camera director, the editor, and finally the composer start coming in and familiarizing themselves with the film in conversations and visits with Fellini. Fellini seems to be moving in his work, building up a film, not according to a chronological progression of the various production phases, but from a permanent central point in a closed circle.

17

Penus the Magician

DURING THE PREPARATION of a Fellini film, something always happens which is on the cusp between experiment and farce, the half-meant and joke. For instance, in *Satyricon*, there was a nighttime excursion on the Via Appia Antica. Fellini, Bernardino Zapponi, and I were guided by Penus, a medium and clairvoyant. Our aim was to make contact with the ancient Romans.

At 10 P.M., using two cars, we left Piazza del Popolo. When we reached our goal out in the open country, halfway up the famous tourist road, it suddenly began to drizzle lightly. During the brief trip, the driver had already personally experimented with Penus's clairvoyance but was not convinced. So he now made the wise decision to dine in a nearby *trattoria*. The magician's secretary, taciturn, melancholy, and a bit sinister, wouldn't even get out of the car. He was quite indifferent to what by now must have become a routine devoid of surprises. On the other hand, Fellini, Zapponi, and I strode forth in the pitch darkness. Every step of the way, we risked breaking an ankle or cracking our skulls on an invisible ruin or capital. Then, all we did for three-quarters of an hour was to hop, skip, and jump from place to place, halting according to the demands of the spiritualist water-diviner, Penus, in the shelter of a mausoleum ruin or a totally profane boulder. We promptly stood in a circle for the fateful chain, our heads together, our hands entwined, like the base of a gymnastic pyramid. Fellini alternated among frowning attentiveness, humorous comments, witty bons mots, and insolent questions to the medium. Bernardino, perplexed and complying, tried to overcome his splitting headache with that strange, calm, dry humor of his. I myself oscillated between dull intimidation and detachment, which I desperately tried to make ironic. In Penus's typically hectic verbal delirium, it was hard to distinguish between what was due to the torrent of words and what was due to his waking state. Penus, however, wavered between senseless or indecipherable shreds and detailed descriptions, which were occasionally suggestive or even thrilling, like the entrance of a tired but victorious army into the capital.

All at once, we ran into some dead lions, which had been poisoned as an example of what would happen to a group of Christians if they didn't renounce their faith. For several minutes, Penus had been smelling the presence of those animals somewhere, who can say how deep in the ground. According to a bizarre practice of trance — a kind of law of supply and demand in the supernatural economy — he was raving speedily and anxiously, tossing out orders and questions: "Ask me if the lions are here! Ask me! Are the lions here? C'mon! Ask me! Ask me if the lions are here!" Fellini, skeptical and patient, asked: "Are the lions here?" Penus, placated and now very secure, drily concluded: "No!" At a certain point, there was actually an interference: a Venetian painter of the eighteenth century, Piazetta, who had lived in a house by the Appia Antica for a while.

We drove back to town, frustrated and furtive.

18

Excuse Me, How About the Money?

Punctually, WHEN THEY OPEN the office in which the preparation takes place, a mob of incredible people — actors, character actors, extras — starts flowing in. Generally, the atmosphere of the first few days is one of expectancy, as for an imminent visit or holiday. And the holiday arrives, clamorously — several months of frantic merrymaking on a fixed schedule: from 5 to 8 P.M. daily, hundreds of people file past the tables of the assistants, hand over photographs, and leave.

The same flushed, intimidated faces, with surly looks or stupid frozen grins.

The same questions: "Can I get the photo back? When does the shooting start? What kind of a movie is it? Until when will you be taking people?"

The same topography of types: the aggressive, the timid, the boorish, the distrustful, the presumptuous, the stupid, the likable, the dishonest, the overemotional, the crazy.

The same social typology: the shop boy, the student, the pensioner, the professional, the free-lancer, the specialist in a remote area, the businessman, the ballet dancer, the bartender, the statistics professor, the coiffeur, the waitress, the masseuse, the literature teacher, the "beautiful girl," the "younger daughter," the "family mother," the "wife," the part-owner of a boutique, and finally the "ex's" from all walks of life.

The same repetition of incredible self-praises: mumbled, whispered, hinted, yelled, acted out, mimed.

The same ulterior motives: the farmhand trying to place a film exposé as thick as a Bible. The mathematics teacher from Valtellina who is studying film direction at the Bergamo School of Cinema and would like to watch the shooting. The opera singer who wants to be an extra. The nouveau riche lady who'd like to rent out her thirty-room mansion in Naples for the film. The peddler who presents his own bloodhound, personally trained by him.

The usual imitator: the ex–hotel manager who pulls out his dentures and mimics the voice of the old man in Westerns.

The usual nostalgic: the versatile old juggler who arrives with a suitcase stuffed with yellowed newspaper clippings, résumés, posters.

The usual "case": the sixty-year-old noblewoman married to an embassy official, a hermetic poetess, deaf, with a metal knee, and accompanied by a bald general, retired, who is forced to explain to everyone why the signora cannot sit down, and who acts as interpreter by bellowing into the stolid and smiling profile of the poetess.

The usual ineffable manifestation of pure schizophrenia: It is three in the afternoon. A small, colorless guy manages to sneak, undetected, into the office, where Fellini is alone at this unusual time. The little fellow has a bloated file under his arm, and as though urged to do so, he sits down almost reluctantly before Fellini and declares laconically, in a colorless voice, with his eyes glued to a vital point on the left-hand wall: "After studies and investigations that I have been pursuing for five and a half years, I have come to the certain and irrefutable conclusion — which I can prove with the relevant documents [he points to the file] — that you, Signor Fellini, are a Martian, an extraterrestrial being who comes, as I have said, from Mars. It was my duty to inform you of this. Good evening, Signor Fellini."

The usual polyglot: eight languages including Latvian.

The usual simpleton:

"What about the money?"

"What?!"

"No, I mean, what about the money?"

"Do you mean: are we paying for it?"

"No, no! Do *I* have to pay?"

"What are you talking about?"

"Why, this isn't the first time, you know. I leave a photograph, and the next thing I know, I get a bill for five thousand lire."

The usual unsalvageable: the face of a construction worker, robust physique, thick blond hair, a pure dialect of the Marches. A modest, self-effacing, truly mortified air: "I am handsome, I am athletic, I have a book-jacket face, I studied acting for five years (doesn't Masina have an acting school?). If *I* can't be an actor, then who *can?*"

The usual "friends" of Fellini: cordial, jovial, extremely talkative in evoking the events — nearly all fictitious — that sealed their friendship. These people are usually not interested in the screen. Every time Fellini starts a new film, they pop up and make him an honorary head of some charitable committee.

And then the fleeting personalities who are so isolated in their incredible prominence: the Marchesa di Benpurgo, inflated and bristling like an angry bird, produces a calling-card from the dark, intricate, heraldic tangle of her fur jacket, huge eyeglasses, and hair tousled in her face. The working-class woman cheerfully and disjointedly asks Fellini to direct a spine-tingling suicide attempt.

And all these people want to see Fellini, want to talk to Fellini, and they try to cross the space between the waiting room and his office by alleging the classic "personal reasons."

It's always the same mob that comes running the instant Fellini starts a new film. "Same" doesn't mean a special breed of people, it refers to the everyday sort, hence the most disparate: the kind you see at a rally or at a collapsed house, or watching a strike or going to Frosinone to see the little peasant girl meeting the Madonna.

Fellini, attentive, amused, takes part in this teeming anonymity. He seeks the faces, the personages who by right and necessity will enter the story he wishes to tell as if they absolutely belonged there. It is extraordinary to see how exact, how intuitive Fellini is when identifying the people who pass before him. With a rapid, penetrating, almost intrusive look, he succeeds in detecting each person's true, secret, or past vocation, often given up and almost never recognized.

Every Fellini film requires a very precise anthropological species, or else there has to be clamorous hunt for a particular character, with the motto: "Who has seen him?" In 8½, it was the immense Saraghina. In *Juliet of the Spirits*, it was Bishna the magician. In *Mastorna*, the Slavic race was supposed to form the disquieting human backdrop of the movie. To find these people, we had to go on reconnoitering expeditions that vaguely smacked of the Nazi era: we visited the camps of Slavic refugees in Latina and Naples. For *Satyricon*, the offices were constantly besieged by a rude army of porters from the slaughterhouse and the general market or by transport workers.

When Fellini prepares a new film, he promptly reviews his enormous photo archives, making an approximate selection of the faces he will use. His haste and impatience in wanting to complete the selection at once are probably dictated by his extreme pleasure in destroying the discarded photographs. In the case of *Satyricon*, the photos destined for the slaughtering block numbered at least two thousand, for which he had to ask the help of Oreste, our clerk. Oreste nurtures a silent passion for Fellini. He has an avid, good-natured face, and above all, a head as square as a cutthroat's. At the center of the room, half-buried in the photo cabinet, sweating profusely from the strain of tearing up the pictures, Oreste suddenly raised his square head, turned it slowly toward Fellini, and whispered ecstatically: "You're one of a kind, doc, you sure are!" At that moment, his dedication became the sinister loyalty of the old servant who one fine day cuts his master's throat. However, his comment clearly revealed that for Oreste, the most resplendent, most indisputable proof of Fellini's talent was the operation the clerk was helping with. Oreste lowered his square head and went back to work. Ultimately, at a certain point, he had to be stopped by force. Otherwise he would have ripped up everything and demolished the entire office.

The newness of faces is a crucial demand for every film of Fellini's. And he always falls in love with the same faces. His photo archive, the truly useful and secret one, has not changed for decades. Hence, the trouble, the climate of a police roundup, of a survey of accident victims, when the actors are called. One is in a lunatic asylum, another in Australia, this one in a hospital, that one dead, the next is being hunted by the narcotics squad, another has changed his sex, the rest have changed at least their addresses. Not infrequently, for instance, a delicate adolescent of eight years ago has turned into a sweaty, hairy recruit. Furthermore, this archive is essentially conservative. It can go through catharses, through shattering events (the psychological subdivision of types changes for each film), but it will not tolerate invasions or escapes. This systematic condition for each Fellini film — the newness of faces — cannot be related to the cinema in general: Fellini never goes to the movies. That's why it can happen that he'll insist on a long shot or rear view of an actress who's already garnered two Oscars. Perhaps the notion of new faces does not refer to an external, objective criterion for Fellini, i.e., a truly new face. For him, the unknown is a one-way current flowing by itself, and renewal does not mean accepting an already existing and autonomous diversity. It means reinventing the known: a famous face becomes virginal thanks to make-up, lighting, various roles. Otherwise, the motor of invention in Fellini is always familiarity.

19

But Are You Sure
There Are No Indians There?

DURING THE PREPARATION of a film, Fellini may often abandon one difficult or unrealizable figurative or technical solution and adopt another. For instance, in *Juliet of the Spirits*, Juliet's grandfather has a Wright Brothers flying machine, but the screenplay called for a montgolfier. Clemente Fracassi, the organizer, promptly smelled the difficulty (Fellini would say: disaster) and wanted to take care of the montgolfier himself. Off he went to Zurich in quest of a tiny old man, an illustrious specialist for aerostatic ballooning. After a week, Fracassi came back with a detailed documentation but especially with the absolute conviction that the montgolfier idea had to be given up.

Whenever Fellini talks about the episode, he gives this rather amusing distorted version of Fracassi's doubtlessly sensible objections: "We have to forget about the montgolfier. The whole enterprise is too risky and the cost exorbitant, because if we want to shoot with a sound margin of safety, we'll need at least four montgolfiers. The first can easily be wrecked when it's loaded with ballast. As for the second, we can't be sure that it won't get entangled in the pines of Fregene and suffer the same fate. And the third — who can guarantee that a sudden gale won't sweep it away God knows where with Giulietta, Sandra Milo, the grandfather and the little girl?" Fellini never bothered to explain why Fracassi needed a fourth montgolfier, since the movie could not possibly have continued after its main actors fearfully vanished into the cosmos.

Clemente Fracassi is highly capable and intelligent, but he can sometimes fall victim to that irrational pessimism to which one is condemned by a rationalism that's all too rigorously applied. Fellini, on the other hand, affectionately maintains that his friend is incurably drawn to negative situations, that only catastrophes can attract him, even cheer him up. And the director, with his rare faculty of achieving exactness by means of ingenious improbability, defines his collaborator's professional qualifications as follows: "If I happen to remark offhand to Fracassi that I want to go to Naples, he replies in confusion: 'But are you sure there are no Indians there?' "

20

The Dyspeptic King

THE SCREEN TEST for the actors has a literal sense, though in reverse. Its real goal is to see whether an actor is *wrong* for the part assigned to him. Hence, ultimately, nearly all the actors get different roles from the ones they had in the tests.

For these tests, Fellini never uses important scenes from the film, but only those which he has more or less decided to leave out. It's as though he didn't want to be unfair to those scenes and were paying them a final affectionate tribute.

The first day of the *Juliet* tests went through the chaotic climate of an opera. The shots of the opera were to be telecast inside Juliet's home during the closing sequence of the invaders. Naturally, the finished film has no trace of that initial plan.

The ideal stage for the action was simply the studio floor. The players were old character actors and extras. On the other hand, the imposing, opulent costumes, under whose weight they were staggering, came from Rome's Teatro dell'Opera. The costumes had been lent only after a month of nagging, strenuous efforts, and the use of "pull." The meaning of the opera scene always remained incomprehensible. Only one thing was clear: it took place in a heavily dramatic atmosphere. The actors were placed on the stage in unduly emphatic, desperate poses, some kneeling, some prone, some in the act of fleeing with raised arms, some standing immobile, their hands perilously entangled in their wigs.

The anguished grimaces, the mouths wide open as if singing, greatly increased the terror of the event, which nevertheless remained mysterious. But the following elements, more than any others, gave the whole business a culminating accent of catastrophe: the moment the clapstick clapped, an overwhelming passage from a recording of Bellini's *Norma* exploded at top volume. At the same time, less suggestive but more deafening, an enormous wind-machine began blasting from the side of the alleged stage. Alas, its performance (there was no smaller machine available) went far beyond the call of duty, i.e., beyond the modest symbolism of the narrative situation. The forthcoming wind was so powerful that the actors grabbed wildly at one another to keep from crashing to the ground or being hurled against the back of the studio. Like a sandstorm, the wind blasted up furious clouds of dust and cardboard. Leaves smashed against a tragically uplifted eye, a sneering cheek, or, more frequently, a wide-open mouth, almost suffocating the actor.

Each "cut" was followed by several minutes of lugubrious calm, the kind that comes after an earthquake or cloudburst. But Fellini ruthlessly pressed on with yet another take.

An ancient German lady, heavily bedizened as a king, had taken a potent laxative the night before. Every half hour, they had to lower "His" Majesty from the lofty throne where she perched with the queen, and then she was brought to the toilet. Furthermore, the two sovereigns wouldn't stop fighting because, since they sang in different languages, they kept confusing each other. The "king's" restless intestinal needs were the sole occasions for pauses during that tempestuous day.

The constructions, phantasmic in the darkness of the studio, are finished.

The actors have been cast.

The team has been formed.

Now Fellini can get on with that splendid, uninterrupted screen test which each film of his constitutes.

Unless . . .

21

The Voyage of G. Mastorna

THE DIFFICULTIES, the vicissitudes of a Fellini film were sometimes resolved only by not making the film. This was the case with the now legendary *Voyage of G. Mastorna.*

Was this something more than or different from an unmade film?

Perhaps we can start by saying what the movie was *not.* It was not, for instance, the obscure cause so much as the evident victim of the extraordinary span of time, about three years, that its impossible birth required. Nor was it mysteriously responsible for an infinite series of events ranging from the dramatic to the grotesque. It merely constituted their outer alibi.

For Fellini, things were different. His fantasy, his gift for deforming reality, a certainly irrational but totally unsuperstitious behavior, his subliminal and inalterable sense of guilt, which often forces him to deny any responsibility, any authorship — none of these things can be satisfied with banal evidence, with opaque objectivity.

The film was an exploration of the other world, the wanderings of a man after death. Hence, it was intangible material, forbidden terrain; and from the very start, Fellini identified it with a fatal entity, both artful and cheerful.

One day, Fellini and Dino De Laurentiis decided to do the film together. Not only was it never made, but it gradually distilled such a quantity of toxins and viruses that for a long time it survived, paradoxically, only in terms of its constant and active state of self-destruction. Rigorously listing the events, episodes, misunderstandings that animated the stormy relationship between Fellini and the Neapolitan producer would be like performing an absurd and actually rather boring tarantella. Furthermore, it could spark an attempt at judging in favor of either party. But that would be thoroughly useless, and only an infantile or partisan mind would want to go to all that trouble.

Creation requires a constant participatory tenderness, an assent that is convinced but firmly rooted in common sense. By his very nature, Dino De Laurentiis is the type of industrialist who programs his products from top to bottom and marks out their destiny without a second thought, using the people involved — no matter what their level — as instruments. When the entire film clique moved to the marvelously equipped offices and studios on Via Pontina (Fellini dubbed them the "giant snake"), the director started drooping like a plant in a refrigerator. Dino De Laurentiis actually put a red stamp on Fellini's advance checks: WAITING ARTIST.

The Voyage of G. Mastorna was a film offering very little to the usual speculative greed of producers. Now this relationship was already precarious enough. And to make matters worse, Fellini had been afflicted for some time with a paralyzing confusion, which drove him to uncertain renunciation or useless, implacable stubbornness. In normal conditions, his vitality would have overcome all obstacles. He would have made the film he wanted to make, the way he wanted to and where he wanted to. But in a state of depression like the one he was suffering from, he could do nothing but defend himself, even at the price of complete immobility.

Finally, the basic strains in the Fellini–De Laurentiis relationship led to a first clamorous rupture. Fellini's innocence was downright provoking. Here is its sorrowful expression, more definitive than any accusation or rebellion:

> Rome, September 4, 1966

> Dear Dino,
> I have to tell you about my internal struggle, which has been going on for some time now and which has finally come to a conclusion.
> This is a serious decision, which I do not wish to dramatize, but it is the only honest reply to my mind, which is worn out with useless and repeated efforts to placate deeper and truer frames of mind by employing reasons suggested purely by a feeling of friendship. I cannot begin the film because after all the things that have happened, I will not be able to complete it. Do not misunderstand me: I have no doubts as to the film itself. But there have been so many contradictory, disturbing incidents, which have nothing to do with the film but which have surrounded the birth and course of the preparations with an atmosphere of resistance and stagnation. All this has alienated and exhausted me, and there is no way I can make my film in such conditions.
> I would like to prevent any distressing personal situations for either of us and any unnecessary external consequences. Moreover, I really need a little peace and solitude. Therefore, I ask you, in all friendship, to deal with Giorgio De Michele, whom I have entrusted with everything.
> I hope that the friendship and esteem confirmed by the long history of our relations will enable us to find some way of resolving the problem.

> I am truly sorry, dear Dino, that I have reached
> this conclusion, but I cannot do otherwise. I em-
> brace you and I wish the best of luck.

Fellini's disarming sincerity triggered a furious reaction from De Laurentiis.

There were intimidations, quarrels, legal attachments. In Modena, an admirer of Fellini's offered him two nets and four mattresses. The newspapers, zealous as ever, helped turn the break into a raving mess. Certain statements, attributed to the two men and headlined on the front pages, seemed like funny typographical errors. De Laurentiis's ardent invective, "I want to cleanse the Italian cinema!" sounded like a Salvation Army slogan. Fellini's answer, "Cut the crap!" quivered with the grim irritation of a Chicago gangster.

After that, for four months, *The Voyage of G. Mastorna* was bandied around by half the world like a roll of mortgage-ridden cloth by a bunch of eager but incompetent salesmen.

December brought the possibility of a production with the participation of a newly formed distributor, Italnoleggio. This was a government institution, under direct Socialist aegis, for producing and distributing films. *Mastorna* thereby became a kind of battle standard, a Marxist-Leninist revolutionary instrument to launch the overthrow of our political and social system.

At rallies during that period, one could hear the battle cry: "Down with the system!" Which meant the capitalist system of the Italian motion picture.

However, the system did not go down, because at the last moment, Federico Fellini, who was not part of the system, gave up on Marcello Mastroianni as lead for the film. This provoked the withdrawal of American funds from the combine, which collapsed ignominiously.

Fellini lost both his patience and his temper. But ultimately, he began practicing his fakirlike knack for adjusting to even the most uncomfortable or burdensome reality by turning everything into an entertainment, a spectacle, disintegrating everything with an inexhaustible humor that was both tender and pitiless, lucid and sympathetic. He even gave himself a precise role: the incorrigible gambler up to his ears in debts, whom a motley bunch of friends and racketeers is trying to drag out of the mess. Or else the jobless man with daily problems of scraping out a living. I recall that one morning he came from Fregene with a package containing two or three gold brooches and a small medallion. This incredible nest egg was sold to a jeweler on Via del Tritone, and the cash allowed Fellini to take a friend out to lunch: Hans Richter, the famous painter and Dadaist.

All attempts at putting *Mastorna* back on its feet ultimately floundered. Then, mysteriously and ineluctably, who should turn up again but De Laurentiis. They came together one evening, and their powwow had the reserved and cautious tones of a Mafia parley — as Fellini said later on. The producer, the director, and his lawyer sat down in a car, closely tailed by De Laurentiis's empty automobile, which contained only his chauffeur. For about an hour, the two vehicles glided slowly and silently through the dark labyrinth of tiny streets in Villa Borghese.

The result was a dismal, unnatural reconciliation.

Fellini went back to work, in good form, even in a good mood. But the later events retrospectively made his behavior look like some sinister goodwill. With a slightly feverish irony, he kept fantasizing more and more about imminently retiring from the cinema. He would then open a couple of haberdasheries or hardware stores and settle down in Fregene. Yet recently, he had been nurturing a sort of fear of this place, which seemed to represent stagnation and isolation.

Then came the explosive high point. Fellini froze into an automaton. He lost any real enthusiasm after Ugo Tognazzi was cast as Mastorna, the part for which Laurence Olivier had been seriously considered. The tremendous disparity between the two actors betrayed the director's tormented confusion about the character. Nevertheless, he managed to transform his basic uncertainty into judicious dialectics: "Laurence Olivier has a stupendous face, but he would not be credible as Mastorna. His face has a peaceful spirituality, a deep, calm intelligence, the detachment of a man who has comprehended everything and grown familiar with the thought of death, overcoming it or merely giving it a suitable place inside himself. By the end of the film, G. Mastorna could have Laurence Olivier's face, but not earlier. Prior to that, I would feel useless, listless with an actor like him. Ugo Tognazzi's face, on the other hand, is fraught with nostalgia and presentiment, with confused desires. It can be more stimulating for me, it can give me the energy and enthusiasm necessary to sweep me along or let me accompany that man on such a perilous trip."

Countless and highly diverse performers were thought of for the part — from Gregory Peck to Eli Wallach, from Paul Newman to Oskar Werner, from Omar Sharif to Danny Kaye and Peter O'Toole, from Vittorio Gassman to Enrico Maria Salerno. But instead of making the character more individual, they seemed to turn Signor Mastorna once and for all into a standard, a universal type, so that by now, anybody could have played the part.

However, given its internal structure and profound motives, *The Voyage of G. Mastorna* could not tolerate such a dissolution of the individual features of its protagonist. Of course, such a dissolution could be an inevitable, natural process in Fellini the author, as shown by later films, *Toby Dammit* and *Satyricon*, in which the performers are reduced to the splendid generality of the most emblematic objectivation. Perhaps that was the point at which the reasons for the long crisis of *Mastorna* were identified with the premises for a new creative phase for the author.

Before the casting of Ugo Tognazzi, Fellini had toyed with the possibility of using a clown. Not only that, but clowns could have played the two other important characters in the movie: Armandino the Neapolitan and Professor De Cercis. And indeed, the same clown could have done all three parts — parts that were the psychological dissection of a single person.

Now Ugo Tognazzi certainly didn't have the metaphysical melancholy or the delicate irony of a clown. Still, he was a comedian and, above all, very far from any romantic, idealistic characterization of a tormented, introverted, spiritual Mastorna. A characterization that, for my money, had a strongly conventional, even reactionary streak.

Despite his great temperament, Tognazzi certainly had nothing of a young Werther about him. Quite the contrary. His physical appearance was vaguely simian. However, Darwin's scientific impartiality, I told myself, is always better than a racism of the mind.

One Sunday afternoon, Ugo Tognazzi presented himself at Federico's home in Fregene. The actor was enshrouded in a black cape — the kind worn even today by certain peasants. A slouch hat perched on his head and each hand clutched the legs of a squawking chicken.

The incredible masquerade and its inscrutable reasons amused, confused, and touched Fellini. The flashing vision of a peasant Mastorna was an unbearable hallucination, a presage.

Fellini got sick.

He was taken to the hospital at night with terrible pains in his chest. He was suffering from pleurisy and anaphylaxis. At first, a lot of people did not believe that his stay in a hospital was really necessary. They suspected it was a good excuse, a rather childish way of escaping *Mastorna,* De Laurentiis, and Tognazzi. I registered their distrust with the friendly superior awareness of a person who knows how true, in a figurative sense, certain gross thoughts of an idiot may be.

Fellini, pale, drained, leaning on a mountain of pillows, the sinister oxygen tubes in his nostrils, the hypodermoclytic needle in his forearm, had to do what De Laurentiis did whenever uttering the name of Mastorna: conjure away Neapolitan spirits.

Luckily, Fellini recovered from his pleurisy and anaphylaxis. Not only that, but he also recovered from *Mastorna.* The violent trauma of the illness and its long course seemed to pulverize three years of conflicts, hostilities, difficulties, tensions. Fellini emerged detoxified, reconciled with everybody and everything, full of new energies, perhaps with fewer illusions, fewer childlike enchantments, yet enriched by a more fertile, more severe contact with reality.

During his convalescence in Manzina, near Rome, he de-

ts for the unmade film *The Journey of G. Mastorna*

voted himself to a project that chimed marvelously with his slow emergence from a regressive state, his rebirth, which is the usual toll of a long and serious illness. He amused himself by sketching events, people, landscapes that had fascinated him in his childhood. The little drawings were to illustrate a long chat about Rimini, the main part of a book on his city, to be published by Cappelli.

Fellini's relationship to his hometown is rife with obscure, contradictory feelings. He is tied to Rimini by a kind of enslavement that alternately enraptures and repulses him. Now, for the first time, he approached Rimini directly and securely, with no more fear, rites, or aversion. And his writing, speaking, and talking about it were similar to those of a man who can finally stare into the eyes of the sphinx, consciously to verify, as an adult, her nurturing, but also imperiling and imprisoning sap — and not to love her again or love her more, or to destroy her, but to return her to her natural dimension, which is that of a perennially consoling actuality and continuation.

For a short time, there were more skirmishes, accusations, extortions, like the final intolerable aftereffects of an ugly nightmare that has come to an end. Then Fellini confronted De Laurentiis, showing a persuasive force that was no longer his own, but determined by the reality in which both men were trapped. With his wonderful gift of simplification, with that wealth of good sense that he sometimes reveals, Fellini said more or less the following to the Neapolitan producer: "Listen, Dino, let's have a very objective look at our situation. For three years now, you and I have been bleeding one another white to make a movie that we still haven't managed to get off the ground. This means there's something wrong, something amiss in our relationship, and it could easily doom us both to being dangerously unproductive. To safeguard our friendship, the only sensible thing we can do is split up and go our separate ways. You release me from my obligation to you, and I'll try to restore the money that's been devoured during the ups and down of the film."

This time, De Laurentiis had no choice but to give in. Not because this new difficulty found him unprepared or exhausted,

but because, perhaps for the first time, he realized he was facing something that eluded him, something he couldn't understand. He was overcome not by the opponent's superiority, but
by his alien being.

The ceremony of dissolving the contract deserves to be retold
briefly.

It was late at night. In Dino De Laurentiis's immense, incredibly luxurious office at Castel Romano, you could hear only
the humming of the air conditioner. The lawyers for both parties gathered in a corner of the room to put the final touches on
the dissolution. Fellini sat absentmindedly at the large table
where the meeting was taking place. Dino De Laurentiis nervously pretended to be leafing through some magazines. He
had a bitter and angry expression on his face. Luigi De Laurentiis, his brother, was pacing up and down the room, constantly
gazing at Fellini with inquiring, almost astonished eyes, as
though he didn't quite understand what and whom it was all
about.

Every so often, some difficult, incomprehensible legal term
would rebound from the group of lawyers: reciprocal usucapion,
via compulsiva. Each term, like a mysteriously whispered counterpoint, sliced through the ostinato of the air conditioner. With
the generosity of a prisoner about to regain his freedom, Fellini
gently said to Dino: "You see, Dino, you and I were stuck in a
hole. . . ." The words dissolved in the humming air. The producer asked with a frown: "What hole?" Fellini stood up,
walked over, and went on: "We were stuck in a hole. What else
can we do but join hands to get out?" De Laurentiis gazed at
Fellini uncertainly for a moment, then said with restrained irritation: "You sure get over things fast!"

The *Mastorna* notebook concludes with the following statement: "Try to give up the fight halfway through the film, as
though the very idea of the story of Mastorna's voyage had the
ill-omened and reasonable power to paralyze its author's creativity. Everything is blocked; everyone, even the public, is
struck by this paralysis. Death is something so unknown that
the sheer notion of speculating about it is senseless and wildly
presumptuous. The wall of the eight-story railroad car collapses

on the platform of the station built in the studio. HALT!
ADJOURNED! TILL WHEN?"

The process of adjourning *Mastorna* may already be finished.
In this case, its author's interrogative "when?" is replaced by
the real "where?" of his subsequent films.

22

In Search of Toby Dammit

EDGAR ALLAN POE, the father of American literature, the
poète maudit, the genius drunkard who, in his perennial ethyl
coma, managed to express, with the prodigious lucidity of extreme and irreversible states, the most secret deliriums, the
most terrorizing compulsions of human nature — Edgar Allan
Poe entered Fellini's existence like a sort of very loving tutelary
god. His dark apparition coincided with a series of very happy
events: the complete recovery from the illness; the definitive
abandonment of *Mastorna*, and — last but not least — the
meeting with Bernardino Zapponi, Fellini's newest friend and
scriptwriter.

I wouldn't be surprised if Fellini kept a picture of Poe in his
wallet, the pale effigy of a living corpse, the way some people
carry around an amulet or the tiny portrait of a saint.

The theater in which these events took place, intercrossed,

and amalgamated was Fellini's small office, the first he'd ever had. For years, often with a born vagabond's lack of conviction, he fantasized about having an office all his own, a tranquil place for meeting friends, collaborators, acquaintances. But distracted and lazy as I was, and trusting to his great adaptability, I had always kept putting off any serious hunt for an office. Besides, we had managed to endure our restless existence as nomads through the various production offices with which we had to grapple from time to time, the hall of the Plaza, a corner in the Caffè Greco, and so on.

Finally, profiting from the last vestiges of his convalescence, Fellini made up his mind: an office had to be found. And now here we were: number 27, Via della Fortuna, three small rooms, a kitchenette, and a bath, in an old building in the center of town, belonging to the Mekhitarist monks, who have their mother house in Venice. It took all the amused patience of a policeman, which Federico sometimes musters, to locate the administrator, Father Samuele, who had withdrawn far away to a deep meditation.

In this little office, on an old, climbing street, who should enter one day but Edgar Allan Poe in the guise of Les Films Marceau. The French producers suggested that Fellini do an episode based on Poe's "The Telltale Heart." The other two episodes in the package movie — "William Wilson" and "Metzengerstein" — would be directed by Louis Malle and Roger Vadim. Fellini did not turn the offer down immediately, even though the resumption of *Mastorna* for De Laurentiis seemed imminent. He wanted to think about the idea. I'm almost certain that this was a case of his habitual incapacity for definite, reasonable, and responsible decisions, his willingness to let events wash up to and over him. He never pushes the events away himself, he merely lets them be replaced by other events, old or new. It's a kind of equilibrium game, which seems as random, natural, and necessary as a chemical compound.

He didn't even read the Poe story. *I* read it.

Meanwhile, to furnish the new office, he went to a poor carpenter on the outskirts of Rome. Desks, shelves, closets in teakwood, efficient and anonymous; a living room, likewise in teakwood, with huge, square foam-rubber cushions in black and yellow slipcovers. "That's fine like this, isn't it? If we spent too much time selecting the furniture, if it were too precise and personal, I'd find it annoying. Anonymity, on the other hand, doesn't obligate you in any way, it doesn't suggest or impose any state of mind or particular mood. You feel totally free. And besides, the furnishings make me feel good."

"The Telltale Heart" didn't interest him, he found it too meager and too Grand Guignol. But he didn't throw in the sponge. He began a dizzying pillage of Poe. One, two, three, four complete editions of his stories. After a week of uninterrupted reading, I was utterly dazed. I felt as if I were floating through an emaciated crowd of living dead, moving and breathing among terrifying apparitions of macabre heroines. My reports to Federico seemed like those of a sick woman confessing to exhausting aberrations and madnesses.

Fellini's typical, purely superficial impatience (a disquiet expressed in concrete motions, for basically he has a patience second to none) — Fellini's impatience in those days reached unheard-of climaxes, like comical gags. He made out entire checkbooks with the mechanical voracity of a sleepwalker.

The rosary of Poe's tales was at an end. Fellini was fascinated by the opening scene of "The Assignation" because it lends itself to a highly suggestive figurative composition. The Grand Canal lit up by torches, the pale, stony face of the noblewoman in an evening gown, staring at the watery surface where her little son has vanished, sailors, gondoliers, urchins, hunting through that black well, the long dive executed from the roof of a palazzo by a black silhouette shrouded in a cape, looking like a giant bird of night. But you can't make a thirty-minute episode with a single frame.

For all of a Sunday, Federico liked the idea of doing "The Angel of the Odd." A series of clean, exact little pictures, as in the children's section of the *Corriere della Sera*. But then he realized that every image would have to be reconstructed in the studio, because the actions and settings were so unusual that they couldn't be filmed in real life.

Now "Never Bet the Devil Your Head" popped up for the
first time. Fellini waxed enthusiastic for two whole minutes
over the final scene of the story: the covered bridge across the
river out in the country, the dark, lame manikin, with the
shiny, evenly parted hair, placing Dammit's rolling head in his
short black satin apron and then hobbling away without turning.
But what about the rest of the episode?

When I gave Fellini the summaries of the stories I had read,
I was ill at ease, disoriented. His definite, although ephemeral
reactions gave me an unpleasant sensation, as though I would
be held responsible for any catastrophe. Still, I was calmed
down by the comforting impression that if Fellini didn't read
Poe's stories himself, then the whole business was still in flux
and not all that important. Next, the matter became very concrete, it acquired its own weight, but Fellini still hadn't read
and wouldn't read a single tale by the American writer. His
knowledge of Poe went back twenty years. Yet not even this occasion, which was basically obligatory if not downright stimulating, could make him go more thoroughly into that author.

Although he wasn't really all that excited about filming Poe,
Fellini did not break off with the French. On the contrary, he
went through the various phases of negotiations with a loving
kindness that balanced his annoyance at the object of the negotiations. He even started thinking about a possible expressive
mode for filming the episode. And he actually went so far as to
sign a true and proper contract with the Paris producers.

For Fellini, such a rash, reckless, unconsidered action is
quite normal. When he's not working, he spends all his time
signing contracts, options, weaving a whole network of obligations, deadlines, motives for professional commitments: he is
trying to give his own lazy and unpredictable character an appearance of discipline, a suitable programming.

By now, the office on Via della Fortuna was completely fur-
nished. Fellini, placated at last, often gazed about, thoughtful
and tender, seeking to understand what it resembled, hunting
for a definition. But his comment, joined by a cheerful laughter,
was always the same: "My organizing talent, my activity are
prodigious only if I apply them to absolutely useless en-

terprises." In point of fact, the only sure characteristic of this
office is its serene and delicate quality of enigma. It could be almost anything: an eccentric house, an address registered to no
one, an untenanted caprice, a branch of a company for reindeer
hides, the modest, respectable front for a drug dealer. The lack
of any daily necessity, any concrete justifying purpose, makes
the place a kind of existential state, or a metaphysical dimension, where you go to think, to rest, or to vanish.

But what about Poe? What story should be chosen?

As always when he's undecided and his doubts and uncertain-
ties have pushed him into a basically uninteresting situation,
Fellini began to complain. He was as troublesome as a child
who can't stand any sort of malaise because he doesn't understand it, or as grumpy as an old aunt who refuses to explain her
malaise so that she can keep on complaining. At such times,
Fellini is irritated with everyone, and on this particular occasion, he was annoyed at Poe, at the French producers, and
above all at himself.

His solitary and indirect quarrels with Poe, generally speaking, became a sensible lament, yet it was quite comical since no
one was forcing him to anything: "Now just tell me, what sense
does it make to film Poe? Apart from the fact that such trans-
plants, such associations are always unnatural and ill-fated, Poe
is such a great writer that his language is a perfect unity in
which the images and their meanings permeate and illuminate
one another. To remove Poe from his written word, especially
today, after the experiences of Existentialism, Surrealism, and
psychoanalysis, would be arbitrary and uninteresting, it would
kill any attraction in the two fantastic intuitions and constructions. And what about translating him literally? In that case,
Mario Bava is the most qualified man, he would be the most
rigorous and suitable director for the job."

He was far more drastic and aggressive with the producers:
"*Edgar Allan Poe as Seen by Federico Fellini* sounds like a publicity blurb, a slogan made up by stupid and vulgar movie busi-
nessmen."

Someone might say to him: "Listen, Federico, why are you
making things so hard on yourself? All you really have to do is

film a twenty-five-minute episode. That's pretty trivial, relatively speaking. So don't kill yourself trying to work up a total commitment and enthusiasm. Make the episode as well as you can, like the skillful moviemaker that you are." To which he retorted: "It's not a question of length, of twenty-five minutes or an hour and a half. It's not a question of commitment or enthusiasm. The real problem is to establish whether or not you like a thing, whether it appeals to your imagination or leaves you cold. And I don't much feel like making this episode. It's like wanting to have sex without being able to."

So you change your tune: "Listen, Federico, you won't succeed in doing something if you don't feel a rapport with it, if it doesn't grow out of your needs, if you don't basically believe in it. So don't give in to the illusion that you're working exclusively on a detached professional level. Put your mind at ease, drop the whole project, and go back to *Mastorna* right away."

But he countered polemically: "No! On the contrary! I'm stupid and presumptuous to boot. I'm not happy unless I go through long, wearying, autonomous creative phases every time. If a man is alive and vital, he'll make everything he touches alive and vital. And besides, all that counts is *doing*. Everything else is words, literature, or intellectual argument."

At such moments, Federico makes you want to take him in your arms and calm him down, for his human weaknesses have the skittish, even slightly futile movements of a shy, insecure adolescent.

I personally believe that Fellini's malaise during that time was nothing but a reluctance to leave a state of indolent leisure without duties, obligations, or responsibilities, in order to go back to a real work routine.

Quick and clear, like lightning that instantly vanishes back into the darkness, came the idea of filming "The Scythe of Time." "I'll get Margaret Rutherford to play the old lady, and I'll shoot the episode on location, in Siena and in the Cathedral of Siena." An equally lightninglike change of mind: "But then again. . . . No, it's like an incongruous and delicate foreshortening of a dream. And besides, it's not really a story, it's just a pretext for Poe to latch on to certain literary fads of the time."

And now the unexpected came on the scene, and its name was just as mysterious: *Gobal*. This was the title of a collection of short stories by Bernardino Zapponi. His stories were terse, precise, and their atmosphere was absurd, grotesque, Kafka-esque. Goffredo Parise, who had written a brief preface to Zapponi's little volume, spoke about it to Fellini, suggesting he read it. Fellini promptly fell in love with a story called "There Is a Voice in My Life." He rang up Zapponi and went to see him. And guess where he lived! Right across the street from our office on Via della Fortuna. Such coincidences can send Federico into raptures, not so much for an irrational superstition, but for a highly rational, almost self-evident, practical consideration: the ease with which certain events occur and develop is a testimony to their benevolence, to their happy necessity.

Meeting Bernardino Zapponi did not supplant Poe's encumbering presence. But it did mark the beginning of a new collaboration, a friendship both unforeseen and genuine. Zapponi's daily visits to the little office were now as warm as those of a neighbor. Zapponi is about forty years old, with a shy, simpatico face. He moves slowly, he even speaks slowly and comfortably. His tranquil, unshakable sense of humor is not a sporadic function of his intelligence, it's a kind of definitive, documentary state. The final word in any of his sentences, questions, considerations is mysteriously commented upon by a hoarse little laugh, a quick, moist look, as though he were hinting: "I know the true meaning of what I've just said. And now you'll see what happens to you."

With Zapponi's story under his arm, Fellini hurried off to the French producers. He told them the plot with the enthusiasm and the vivid, overwhelming language he employs to persuade, to seduce. The Frenchmen were fascinated, but also taken aback because they no longer knew what movie he was talking about, they couldn't understand what had happened to Poe or what Zapponi had to do with it all. Federico mistook their perplexity for a tacit consent and returned home, bubbling with excitement and ideas. Up sprang an insurmountable obstacle: the rights to "There Is a Voice in My Life" had already been optioned by another Italian director. Federico asked, insisted, asked again, but got nowhere. So he started glancing through Zapponi's book again and found another story he liked: "The Chauffeur." With this second story under his arm, he hurried back to the French. He was like a mounted treasure hunter shuttling between a newly found diamond deposit and the company headquarters, with which he is unable to communicate.

This time the French, having recovered from their previous alarm, issued a curt alternative: either Poe or nothing. This ultimatum can be blamed for anything and everything, but one cannot deny its total legitimacy. At any rate, it prevented the whole business from turning into an endless, ludicrous repetition.

Fellini was mystified. He couldn't fathom what he saw as an obtuse refusal by the producers. "Can you explain what difference it could make to the public whether or not the third episode is by Poe? Aside from the fact that the atmosphere and genre are pretty much the same and wouldn't clash with the other two episodes. And besides, I like Zapponi's story a lot more, I'd much rather film it, and that way I'd do a better job."

Alas, the logic of a genius never coincides with the common sense of normal financiers.

The repercussion of the producers' adamancy was promptly felt. Federico, as if to bait them, veered toward an utterly gloomy and utterly conventional Poe. The story he tackled was "The Premature Burial." And he instantly transformed it into a bloodthirsty farce, to which he devoted the full weight of his imagination. During a leisure hour in the calm, enigmatic atmosphere of the little office, he jotted down a page of notes which he didn't even finish. It contained — one may say — the entire cinematic systematization of the story:

> Setting: NAPLES
> Naturally, not the usual festive loudmouthed ragamuffin Naples of folklore, but the more secret, more hidden, the terrifying Naples. The Naples that frightens me; a cancerous secretion of centuries of ignorance, lowness, superstition, cunning.

AMBIENCES: A huge, beautiful church, a high Baroque cupola, immersed in a jungle of old houses, terraces, balconies, with neon signs on the roofs. The station nearby. The subway. The cablecar. The tunnel with its underground corridors. The fetid sea. Among other possibilities, the protagonist could even think up a coffin-boat, make himself a tomb with a slide directly into the sea, wake up to find himself floating in the ocean. SOS rockets. Rescue.

THE ACTOR: MacRoeny (Mariannini or Sordi?) Make him a squalid sacristan always living among funerals and hence terrified of being buried alive.

In this case, perhaps the episode ought to take place in Rome, or even better in one of the Roman castles (Marino, Frascati, Genzano).

The good things in Poe's story (cinematically speaking)

a) First-person narrative

   CLOSE-UP of the twisted, sweaty madman, speaking, confessing this terror, asking for help, living through all the terrorizing obsession, rambling disjointedly to the audience.

b) Three or four little episodes of premature deaths.

c) The devices he comes up with to escape his coffin and grave in case of a premature burial.

d) The nightmare of the ghost showing me the cemetery, with the open graves.

e) The finale (?) which still has to be found. An

outing in a boat with whores. In case it's
Sordi, the end could possibly be . . .

Producers chase Fellini over land and sea, trying to get him
for a movie. But then, once the contract is signed, they
strangely but understandably feel a vague satisfaction, mixed
with anxiety and distrust, in exerting their power and authority,
constantly, attentively, and eagerly. In fact, Fellini's vitality,
personality, and prestige continually risk overwhelming them
and constricting their role — usually the only determining factor in making a film. Generally, their desire for revenge, often
unwitting, succeeds only in petulant, operettalike scenes that
are exasperated but meaningless.

There is a false legend that makes Fellini out to be a capri-
cious, unpredictable, dangerous director, and it was probably
invented by his producers to magnify their function and exag-
gerate their zeal and effort. Contrary to this myth, Fellini is
obliging, always ready to adopt a new and less costly idea. But
this unexpected disappointment doesn't really placate the producers, it seems to anger them even more.

In this case, Fellini instantly refused to do "The Telltale
Heart," which the producers had suggested. He blithely
launched into a vicarious perusal of Poe's complete works. Not
only that, but with a both naïve and unacceptable initiative, he
picked another author.

Now it was the producers' turn. They knew their trade, of
course, but they also had vindictive feelings. And so they objected that "A Premature Burial" was too complex, too rich, it
might bewilder the audience because it contained three tiny episodes, the three cases of false deaths.

With the willing and realistic mildness of a man accepting a
situation that he has ultimately desired, Fellini jumped back
and pounced upon "Never Bet the Devil Your Head."

"It's a matter of filming, with a little background, the final
scene of the wager and the incident that costs the protagonist
his head. I can do it in three days of shooting and fifteen minutes of film. The whole thing could work like this:

"It's dawn on a Sunday morning, the darkness is slowly dissolving. In a still-illuminated house near Ponte Milvio, you can hear voices, shouts. Two men emerge from the building, chatting about this and that. Walking a short distance behind them are their partners, two women who are combing their hair, freshening their make-up, joking and clowning around. There is the bewildered, euphoric atmosphere of the end of a night of merrymaking. The lights are going out on the streets. Now there is only the abstract, motionless first light of dawn. A small iron scaffolding looms on Ponte Milvio, it is meant to protect a street demolition. One of the men, half in jest, half in drunkenness, says he wants to jump over the small framework of pipes. He innocently makes the bet. It's like a watchword setting off a fateful mechanism. The man jumps, his head leaps away, while his companions watch with incredulous, slightly dazed smiles, which gradually vanish. The devil could be the mechanic dozing in the glass cube of a nearby service station. Or a streetcar driver hurriedly striding across the bridge with his lunch under his arm.

"All in all, a lean, rigorous little story, with a kind of metaphysical terror, like Kafka's 'The Knock on the Door.' "

One evening, while returning from Villa Florio, where he had dined with Bernardino Zapponi, Fellini saw the Ponte dell'Arriccia. A section of it had collapsed a few months earlier. He was fascinated by the clear outline of the towering arcades that vanish in a deep valley of green darkness. The Ponte Milvio dissolved, of course, as in a fade-out. Couldn't the beheading take place here? A madman and a drunk decide to make their car leap from one fragment of the bridge to the other. No more metaphysical terrors. Just the desperate defiance of a candidate for suicide.

Fellini saw Peter O'Toole's picture in a magazine, and the protagonist's features took shape, a precise form. A few work sessions with Zapponi, and the project moved from its endless interregnum of hypotheses and possibilities.

An English actor, a movie star, a prestigious interpreter of Shakespeare, his career now on the decline, arrives in Rome to act in a spaghetti Western.

The dreary necessity of the trip. The unreal, incongruous encounter with an unknown city through the window of an automobile.

The cruel and stupid TV interview. The unreal, nightmarish party in his honor. The nocturnal drive in a powerful racing car, past Roman castles, amid fantastic backdrops sliced by the impassive curiosity of the headlights. The bed and the fateful bravura of the leap from the bridge. All these events have lost the warm normality of life, they have become emblematic, they have acquired the transparency of presentiment for the English actor, they are his inevitable steps toward dying.

Peter O'Toole's lunar mask of an insane, infantile, diabolical Pierrot is the exact counterpoint, the measure, the visible, enigmatic expression of a destiny coming true. After two months of doubts, guesses, choices promptly rejected and then reconfirmed, unsatisfying investigations, sometimes amusing, often polemical, for a story by dear Edgar Allan Poe, all that remained was a title, a bridge, and a wild bet.

"What movie is this? Is it still *Gulliver's Travels?*" That was simply a meaningful and humorous lapse, the most entertaining version of a question that was always the same. The information that Fellini was working on an episode, and that he would do *Mastorna* afterward, left everyone speechless and almost disappointed. Federico Fellini and *The Voyage of G. Mastorna* seemed to have become a timeless cinematic convention.

After only two months of hard work, the office on Via della Fortuna was brutally abandoned for the new offices of PEA on Largo Ponchielli (Alberto Grimaldi was a junior partner in the coproduction along with the French). The brief existence of the small office did not permit us any nostalgia, only a fleeting stupor.

Fellini and Bernardino Zapponi met almost daily to complete the short script for *Never Bet the Devil Your Head*. The two men spoke and talked about everything except the episode. The few discussions they did have about it were merely systematically to subvert Poe's tale, to mortify poor Edgar with the insolent joy of two little boys. They defined the characters, they set up the situations, and a collaboration was founded on a kind of free and easy youthful togetherness that had the sober, almost modest look of spontaneity.

Enzo Provenzale, like a kindhearted gnome, was the soul of the offices on Largo Ponchielli. He had worked on Fellini's first movie, *The White Sheik*, some twenty years earlier. Now, after Fellini's long association with Clemente Fracassi (*La Dolce Vita*, *8½*, and *Juliet of the Spirits*), Provenzale seemed destined to become his new organizer.

It was Provenzale who laid the foundations for filming the episode, who made the initial contacts with collaborators and technicians, who gave the preparations a daily concrete order.

The two biggest problems in preparing *Never Bet the Devil Your Head* were the broken bridge on which the unhappy Toby Dammit (that was the protagonist's name) made his final leap and the actor who was to play the role.

The Ponte dell'Arriccia was too hazardous for location shooting, so it had to be given up. Half of Italy was scoured for broken bridges, and the reports were so detailed that they made the search look like a series of military operations. However, the investigation was fruitless, and the possibility of constructing a studio bridge become a necessity.

Building a bridge for an episode with no further architectural obligations should have been quite free of problems. It required only some common sense. But in walked the person least qualified for such an undertaking, an old friend of Fellini's, Fabrizio Clerici. This man is an excellent painter, an artist with a precise, unmistakable touch. So far, so good. Unfortunately, however, after thirty years of theater and opera, he has no mental elasticity whatsoever, he is uncompromising, he is closed to any necessary revisions, any changes that are indispensable in cinematic work. The collaboration of the two friends lasted exactly twenty days. It was like the disastrous cooperation of two deaf men. Fellini filled whole sketch pads to indicate what he wanted. Clerici scattered stupendous models of totally improbable bridges. Their collapses, their breaks were dialectical themes of opera, of nineteenth-century tragedies. But the detail that most effectively sums up the incompatibility of Fellini and

Clerici was their two voices talking uninterruptedly for endless and useless meetings: Fellini's soft, quiet, persistent voice and the set designer's booming voice, all aquiver with baritone echoes, and so low that it seems to yank down Clerici's entire person. The eyes, the nose, the cheeks plummet, and even his voice would seem astonishingly normal if he turned into a dwarf.

In the end, the painter Vespignani did a model based on Fellini's thousandth, and by now obsessive, sketch. This settled the matter.

The problem of finding an actor was more complicated, and this too was resolved with a substitute. One could say that Federico wrote the script on Peter O'Toole's skin, that is, putting the English actor entirely into the episode. The French producers probably lost some time until they began negotiating with O'Toole. By then, he had accepted other commitments, which made it difficult for him to participate in the Fellini episode. In the end, after reading the script, he flatly turned down the offer. O'Toole instantly recognized himself in the twisted Toby Dammit, and even though he was greatly tempted by the prospect of working with Fellini, he ultimately did think about his career, giving in to purely moralistic qualms. He feared that by agreeing so nonchalantly to play himself in a movie, he could hurt his popularity with the greater public. Federico, who gets more and more stubborn the more a thing or person evades him, dashed off to London. He made the personal acquaintance of Peter O'Toole and fell madly in love with him. The actor stuck him as tender, vaguely eerie, so that every so often he fondled him with the maudlin and attentive affection of a drunkard. Having grown more interested in the British star, Fellini put his all into persuading him. Peter O'Toole, fascinated, captivated by Federico, gave in. He agreed to do the episode. But after three days, his earlier qualms resurfaced, he changed his mind, and he called the director in Rome. The actor gave out a string of shrill noes. The telephone conversation became stormier and stormier. Fellini asked for explanations, he was furious. But to no avail. The great distance, the telephone itself, were solid defenses for O'Toole, protecting him against the director's assaults. With malign satisfaction, the newspapers announced that Peter O'Toole had refused to work with Fellini.

Now began the hunt for a replacement.

For an entire week, Fellini's table withstood an uninterrupted torrent of photographs — dozens of pictures of the most famous actors in the world. He consulted piles of *Spot-Light*, the encyclopedia of movie actors. He screened passages from all the films released during the past three years. Not even *Mastorna* had unleashed such a frantic scramble. In that thicket of names, faces, résumés, there were entertaining dialogues, ridiculous objections and evaluations. Ultimately, the criterion was no longer the characteristics of the personage. Each actor's face was scanned for a psychological disposition for the tragic and babyish jump from the bridge. Richard Burton? No: when he's drunk, he only gets in the way, a sweaty boar that slides under the table and stays there. Marlon Brando? Absolutely not! With that robust ass of a successful man, he wouldn't have the innocence, the callowness for anything that pointless. When he climbs into a car, he knows where he's going, and he gets there safe and sound.

The roster was now reduced to two candidates: James Fox and Terence Stamp. The former, with his long hair and blond fringe, seemed like a wild little girl, a graceful and unknown little animal. The latter had the very beautiful and severe face of a romantic hero. As in a competition left totally to chance, the winner was Terence Stamp.

Fellini's reaction after their first meeting was basically rather ambiguous: "He's like Walter Chiari, a Walter Chiari with a blond wig. He resembles him not so much physically as mentally, psychologically. He has the same energy charge, the same restlessness. The only difference is that Terence made his debut with John Gielgud instead of Wanda Osiris and has done Shakespeare instead of Castellano or Pipolo. Last night in the restaurant, for instance, he went through the most disparate moods. He was comical, then serious, then he laughed again, he joked with the waiters, only to plunge instantly into a long melancholy. He's not sick. He has an unquiet nature, but he's not at all disquieting."

Two days after arriving in Rome, Terence had a make-up and costume test. His long, slender, adolescent body was sheathed in violet satin trousers, a white blouse with a jabot, a black velvet jacket, and a black silk scarf. His face, stiffened in a thick, chalky greasepaint, like a plaster cast and halfway between circus and Elisabethan tragedy, had the wild, vacant look of a man devoured by drugs and alcohol. The tousled hair, very long and very blond, was constantly moistened to simulate the typical sweatiness of a drunkard. A singular upward motion of the right eyebrow, near the nose, gave the blue eyes a wild, insolent stare.

The result of this cosmetic operation on a physical type like Terence Stamp's was a character with a fascinating timelessness, and the incarnation of classic romantic motifs — passion, courage, faith, revolt, death — constantly undermined by elements of a more ruthless, more disenchanted neo-Romanticism: disillusion, insecurity, impotence, angst.

This was the first time that Fellini worked with an actor whom he didn't know at all, who belonged to a different generation. And so it was the first time that the director and his star failed to establish that quasi-amorous complicity, that vivid identification and reciprocal enchantment, that tension similar to a closed circuit, to a wavelength — in short, the qualities indispensable for the birth and growth of a character.

The condition that the actor become the character can, in the best of cases, be translated into a complete expressive operation. In many Fellini films, it has become a reality. And not because of some unforeseen psychotic advantage or some artifice of sorcery, but because the actor picked by Fellini did not interpret the character: in some complicated and ambiguous way, he *was* the character.

In several of his films, Fellini has narrated facts, emotions, inner experiences, recollections from his personal life. Even if he transferred them into the dimension of imagination, of memory or humor, he stripped them of their undepictable individualism, incommunicable and hence insignificant. He gave them the perhaps truest and most total objectification — that of poetry.

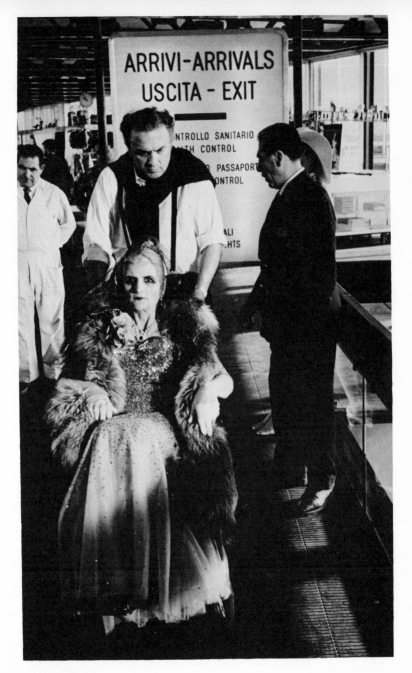

Fellini filming *Toby Dammit*

Edgar Allan Poe, drawn by Fellini

rence Stamp as Toby Dammit

Marina Yaru as the devil in *Toby Dammit*

So if the protagonist of a Fellini film was Fellini himself in
various expressions and nuances, the director could not rely on
a good actor vaguely right for the part and thereby achieving an
actor/character link that was aesthetic or simply true to life.
Fellini was too vitally compromised by such a link, for it could
not become a tension, a confrontation, a verification.

The incandescent three-way situation among Fellini, the
actor, and the character was thus extremely unpredictable and
fluctuating. There was no way of telling anything. Was the actor
supposed to incarnate the abstract, solitary problems that one
Fellini saw in the other Fellini and in the character? The actor's
physical presence, his intervention, were never merely functional, they carried his full creative weight. Didn't that physicality ultimately modify the previously conceived character, didn't
it alter the prior system of relations between Fellini and the
character? Did the physicality become a sort of mirror —
perhaps more limited and binding — of the splendid approximation of self-invention, less attractive than the narcissistic
rigors of self-analysis? Yet the moment Fellini recognized himself, that mirror acquired the provocative and hence illuminating autonomy of a problematic *doppelgänger*.

Even in the daily outer behavior in which it expressed itself,
Fellini's rapport with the protagonist in any film of his was singular or classical for a long time; it depends on whether it is
judged by the professional convention or identified with the
creative reality. Fellini always showed the protagonist a moth-
erly solicitude, wrapping him in a constant tenderness, an avid
interest, offering him an exaggerated, prehensile sensitivity, a
dependence or possessiveness, a natural and intense tyranny.
Whether Fellini listened to or questioned the actor, whether he
baited him or spoke to him, even when the two were simply
together in silence, they both seemed enclosed in the same
magnetic field, they shared the connivance, the solidarity of
people intent on a common effort and experiment.

"Never Bet the Devil Your Head" was not a story by Fellini,
and Toby Dammit was not a creation of his. Hence the necessity of this new rapport with the actor. In fact, the director felt
that if he wanted to preserve the authenticity of Poe's

character — the only possible authenticity — he would have to build up the personage from the outside, not allowing his own subjectivity to interfere beyond the limits of an attentive collaboration. In these terms, the evasive association of Terence Stamp with Walter Chiari, the ironic aims of the hairstyle and make-up for the English actor, the delicate and affectionate reserve between the actor and the director on the set, became precautions, something like a discipline permitting Federico the necessary detachment from Toby Dammit.

A devil had to be found. In Poe's story, the devil was a lame manikin dressed in black. The script made him a slight, blond girl, playing with a ball. All the daily newspapers in Rome ran the following announcement: Federico Fellini is looking for a twelve-year-old girl, blond, pallid, blue eyes, Anglo-Saxon type. For a week, the PEA offices were swamped by clusters of mothers and brothers accompanying squat, florid girls with raven hair. The usual obtuse and aggressive maternal blindness. In the end, Toby Dammit's terrorizing presentiment of death would have the flaxen head, the mysterious, ghostly face of a twenty-two-year-old Russian girl and the wiry little body of a pupil in a dance school.

The costume designer for the film was Pierino Tosi. After refusing the offer to do *Mastorna*, he agreed to do the episode. But during the first few days, he wandered through the offices with the uncertain, desolate air of a man still reassuringly tempted to sneak out the door and escape far away. Fellini's esteem and faith, his insistent affection, rather than heartening Tosi, seemed to disorient him even more. The designer's fear of drawing attention made it appear that he could be serene only in anonymity. His shyness and kindness aroused an instinctive liking, and his talent evoked a protective respect.

The directors for the other two episodes were quite definitely Louis Malle and Roger Vadim. Comically pigheaded, Fellini ignored Vadim. Whenever he had to mention his two colleagues, he always said with embarrassing nonchalance: Malle and Bergman. If someone pointed out the mistake, he would burst out laughing, pretend to think a moment and then, serious once more, say: Bergman.

In this way, he ironically satisfied the people who wanted him to feel an annoyance that he didn't really have.

Two days before the shooting began, Fellini, amid the last-minute confusion, received a telephone call from Dino De Laurentiis. The producer wanted him to do *Waterloo*. If Fellini agreed, the producer was willing to give him a blank check. There is absolutely no comment possible for this event. Nor any kind of judgment. Fascinated and overwhelmed, Fellini said: "I realized that of the two of us, the artist isn't me, it's Dino. Compared to him, I'm sensible, practical, I have the orderly mind of a bank teller."

It took twenty-six days to shoot the Poe episode. Twenty-six confusing days, harried by the foolish hope of respecting the real time in Toby Dammit's very brief adventure.

The editing was almost done. Fellini was dining in a Chinese restaurant with Nino Rota, who has written the music for all his films. All at once, Fellini quoted Poe's stupendous definition of Toby Dammit, from the last part of the tale. The enthusiasm, the excited joy with which Fellini spoke about the American writer could not derive from a random memory. It was more like the fresh emotion of a very recent encounter.

Nino interrupted him: "Excuse me, but that story, didn't you . . . ?"

Federico replied nonchalantly: "I read it yesterday for the first time. It's wonderful."

23

Nino Rota

FEDERICO FELLINI and Nino Rota: when you see them together, they reflect such an extraordinary physical characterization in each other that they seem like two creatures of fable, the mythological and humorous protagonists of an enchantment or ritual. Fellini: big and strong, with a non-stop psychomotoric vivacity, full of inexhaustible tension and curiosity, a highly sensitive and unflinching alertness that overlooks nothing. Nino: short, always absorbed in a distraction that has become his habitual existential state. The sole human signals that Nino transmits from his dimension, i.e., music, are movements having the dreamy vagueness of an unconscious man, a dialogue with frequent rhythms and reasons impermeable to anyone else, a look with the disconcerting firmness of innocence. But this characterization, quite banal if limited to externals, becomes more meaningful, for it precisely expresses the psychological situation. Whether they're at a piano, or in a restaurant, or on the street, Fellini always seems to be leading or following Nino with the protective security of a big brother, with the torment-ing attention of the white clown for August, but also with the avid anxiety of a man waiting for responses and revelations from a small magician in a trance. For Fellini's relation to Nino is his only contact with music, a sort of completed and perfect trans-fer. In this sense, Nino Rota's music, for Fellini, is a fascinating voyage across the moods, events, contents, characters of the director's films. A voyage that is something more than a sugges-tive encounter with Fellini's work, something more profound than a mere emotional examination. For Nino Rota is a testi-mony to his friend's cinematic adventure, a testimony that is perhaps the most unconscious, but for that very reason the most mysteriously lucid and penetrating.

As things stand now, Nino Rota, of all of Fellini's collabo-rators, would seem least apt for and most remote from a direct inquiry into the methods of their collaboration. But there's never a dull moment with Nino. One day, I went to interview him about that very topic. The tenor, the atmosphere, the ca-dences of our meeting were unmistakable, as they always are with a personality like Nino's. Indeed, I feel that I had my own share in that unmistakable quality. Furthermore, his exactness, his precision in talking about his work with Fellini are the very features of a musician. Here is a report on the interview and its result.

QUESTION: I imagine you've always liked the circus too.

ROTA: Yes, it's a spectacle that's always excited me. I remember, once, as a child, I was taken to the Fratellini Circus at Medrano, and I met the Fra-tellinis. I even have a photo of them, all three of the Fratellinis. . . .

QUESTION: Do you still have the photo?

ROTA: Yes. . . . It must be in a scrapbook with the article by the French journalist who took me to see the

Fratellinis. I was in Paris because my oratorio was being performed, my first oratorio. . . .

QUESTION: How old were you then?

ROTA: Eleven. That newspaperman, instead of interviewing me, preferred taking me to the circus, something fitting my age, he was being sort of polemical. . . . But the article he wrote on my debut in Paris was pretty ironic. It sounded as if he were distrustful towards child prodigies!

QUESTION: Do you think that photo of the Fratellinis could still be dug up?

ROTA: I can't find the scrapbook my mother made with all the articles on my first oratorio. It would certainly be amusing to fish out that photo, but I would have to hunt through all my papers. . . .

Maestro Nino Rota got out of the small armchair next to the piano, evidently hoping to search for the photo. Well, there we are, I thought, so much for the interview. Nor could it have been any different, considering what I'd done beforehand. Fellini had suggested: Prepare a series of precise questions, otherwise you'll get nowhere. I didn't prepare them, and so I had to improvise that first question about the circus. It was not only banal, but unfortunate, since I had come a cropper with it. Fellini also advised me to use a tape recorder. I did bring one, but I hadn't checked it out: it was broken. We fooled around with it for three-quarters of an hour, trying to make it work; we had no idea what we were doing. Nino finally called a friend who knows about tape recorders, but you can't do much by telephone. At a certain point, an amused Nino was doggedly and haphazardly banging away at the buttons and switches. I suspected he was trying to knock it out totally in order to avoid the interview. Eventually, we discovered that the thing would function if held in a certain position — a position so bizarre and unnatural that it would irremediably frustrate any foolish hope for a serious interview. So we sat down face to face, settling pon-

Fellini with composer Nino Rota at the piano

Nino Rota, drawn by Fellini

derously into the armchairs, silent and unexpectedly intimidated by the soft hum of the moving tape. Ours was the exaggerated and hence slightly infantile malaise of an interviewer
and interviewee who have little practice with such things.

Perhaps all I could do now was to help Nino look for the photograph. It might make us forget the almost certain failure of
the interview. Unfortunately, Nino promptly began inspecting
the first bundle of sheet music within reach, which meant he
didn't have the foggiest notion of where the photo might be.
But this wouldn't have been so serious if Nino's home, although
consisting of a living room, studio, bedroom, kitchen, bath,
hallway, and one other room, weren't literally buried under
hosts of sheet music, piles of paper, mountains of books everywhere, so that the traditional distinction between various spaces
was no longer possible. Furthermore, even though I wouldn't
let myself be discouraged by Nino's uncertain, intangible ab-
sorption and diligence in searching the apartment, his method
was at least questionable. Not deigning even to glance at them,
he inexplicably ignored trunks and bookcases. Yet for some obscure reason, he insisted on hunting through the same places
over and over again — drawers visibly containing no trace of
any scrapbook and at times even empty. It was clear that for
Nino the interview and the search for the photograph were
subtly and cheerfully mechanical. In reality, he was still thinking of the oratorio he had to finish by the end of September,
when it would be performed in Perugia by the Prague State
Symphony Orchestra. At my arrival, in fact, he had been working at the piano, wearing a striped housecoat over his pajamas.
Inside a closet, we unearthed the music to another oratorio of
his, the Parisian one, a two-part cantata on the childhood of
Saint John the Baptist. For an instant we hoped that the scrapbook would also be nearby. But in this music-filled house, only
the notes obey an intransigent order with mathematical analo-
gies. All we could do was return to our armchairs, hoping that
meanwhile the whimsical recorder had become useful again.
From that point on, the interview progressed rather swiftly, interrupted only by Nino's brief unexplained absences in the bedroom: I later found out that his telephone signals are more tele-

pathic than sonorous. At times, Nino suddenly and rapidly checked to see whether he could locate the Fratellini photo after all.

QUESTION: How did the music to *The Clowns* come about?

ROTA: You know that to guide the film, that is to say, during the shooting, Federico used several passages of classic circus music, for instance "The March of the Gladiators" and "Barnum Circus," or other famous musical pieces like "Ebb Tide" in the finale and "A Night on Bald Mountain" for the strong woman in the childhood circus. Then, when the shooting was done, Federico telephoned me at Bari and said it was time to think about the music. That same evening I sat down to work and composed three or four things that went into the film unchanged.

QUESTION: Had you already seen any rushes?

ROTA: Yes, sometimes. But the sheer idea of doing circus music instantly fired my imagination. The first piece I did that evening was the short march that is the leitmotif for the movie. The second was a tango that accompanies the Fratellini sequence. The third was that sad little background music for the memorial to Dario and Bario. Then, when we met in Rome, Federico, with his usual clarity of mind, had already prepared an overview, a set of musical material that could serve for the film. "The March of the Gladiators" and "Ebb Tide" were discarded. Other things were added: "Fascination," "Io cerca la Titina," and so on. Next, during the actual sketching of the music, we realized we could easily adopt passages from Federico's earlier films, things relating clearly to the circus: the little march in *8½*, the circus in *Juliet of the Spirits*, the nightclub in *La Dolce Vita*. Furthermore, we also thought of using a couple of pieces that had become standards at the circus: "The Ride of the Valkyrie" for the scene with the strong woman, and "The Toreador Song" from *Carmen* for the costume battle. Ultimately, we tried to unite all that heterogeneous material so that there wouldn't be any breaks or imbalances among my three pieces, the already-existing passages, and the ones from Federico's movies. I feel that the final result was very precise and exact. The music to *The Clowns* sounds like real circus music.

QUESTION: Does your collaboration with Federico always follow the same precise course, always repeated in the same way?

ROTA: Yes, generally. To a certain extent, I always know what Federico is doing, I follow his work as far as I can by attending the shootings and looking at the rushes. Then, Federico decides it's time to establish the music — and that always happens before he's done shooting, because by that time, Federico already fairly well knows the direction, the musical tone of the film. Now I start preparing my own ideas, musical hypotheses that I submit to Federico when the film is done. At this point, Federico may instantly accept all the themes that I've prepared, or else the two of us — I at the piano and he next to me — start developing further ideas from my first ones in order to get at what he wants. For instance, this is what happened with 8½: I had already jotted down the first part of the main motif of the film, then Federico and I together found the second part, which ultimately came to dominate.

At other times, however, things went differently because we had decided at the very start to use only existing music. That was the case with *La Dolce Vita* and *Satyricon* — we almost prohibited ourselves from preparing our own material. Then, for *La Dolce Vita*, the music practically emerged on its own. The themes were born of their force — I might almost say while we were recording them.

QUESTION: I'm curious about one thing: Where did you get the famous motif of *La Strada?*

ROTA: Well, I have to say that the theme for *La Strada* was sort of the result of my arrogance. During the shooting, Federico had used a piece of Corelli's, a variation, to guide the film, All of Giulietta's movements had been adjusted to it with the trumpet and all of Matto's with the violin. Federico liked that piece especially and maybe he even wanted to keep it for the sound track, but I couldn't agree with him, I felt it wasn't right for the movie. So I prepared a motif almost along the same rhythmic lines as Corelli's piece, and that was the theme of *La Strada.* You could call it an artificial motif, but it's not always so easy to distinguish things that emerge spontaneously from things that are fabricated, because the two often replace one another or coexist. In any event, the *La Strada* theme sounds anything but artificial.

QUESTION: You composed the music for all of Fellini's films from *The White Sheik* to *The Clowns.* How did you two get to meet?

ROTA: Before *The White Sheik*, we knew each other only by sight. We had in fact met a couple of times before that, because I had written the music for some films based on Federico's scripts. But that was all. We really met for *The White Sheik*, and probably neither Federico nor I ever suspected that this meeting would be so profitable, so beneficial to both of us. . . . A musical *coup de foudre*. . . . And not just musical, because we formed a friendship that has gotten stronger and stronger over the years.

QUESTION: You've worked with all the major Italian directors. Who is your favorite?

ROTA: That's an indiscreet question, which I could answer personally, without that microphone. But it's hard being objective about such questions. Any answer is nearly always determined by elements that have nothing to do with the work itself — for instance: personal friendship, rapport, a more spontaneous way of working. From an exclusively professional viewpoint, I succeeded in doing the music for several films without ever knowing the director. In these cases, I had to rely completely on myself. Naturally, a collaboration as with Fellini, which is so spontaneous, so vital, so natural, always inevitably gives birth to something new, something far more original from the standpoint of film music. Not to mention that in such conditions even the concrete work becomes more joyful, less difficult.

In this respect, let me tell you about one of the most entertaining facets of our collaboration. Federico is always thoroughly convinced that I don't know the film, or that I'm not following it when I see it, or that I confuse it with something else. Yet our rapport is so deep that he never has any doubts whether I can write the music demanded by the film. My distraction has become a recurrent part of our work together. Actually, Federico is right. I'm often distracted, and sometimes I don't see things in the film, or else I see things that don't exist or that are totally different from what's really there. In *The Clowns*, for example, there's a cannon shaft that the strong man lifts on his shoulders in the childhood circus. But I confused it with a mattress. And I recalled two of the mock-up horses as elephants.

Naturally, distraction is a luxury that I can indulge in only with Federico. There are many films I have to see by myself, and so I have to pay strict attention, because later on nobody will confirm whether the music works or not. In such cases, I do actively what I can allow myself to do passively with Federico.

QUESTION: Once, I heard you say that if possible you'd like to have Fellini collaborate on the music you write for other movies as well. How come?

ROTA: One of the qualities I appreciate most in Federico is his clarity of thought. He always knows exactly what he wants as a musical equivalent of an image, and when you play something for him, his reactions, his responses are always precise and definite. Furthermore, he knows how to make things simple, he can make the most complicated and indefinable things so concrete and precise. In a word, when he hears a theme, a musical cue, the immediacy of his emotions, together with his utter accuracy, is a very, very rare quality.

QUESTION: Is that why you two manage to work out the music for a film so rapidly?

ROTA: Federico and I complete the music for a film so quickly that it's better to keep the speed a secret! For propriety's sake, I'd rather not let the cat out of the bag. Especially, if we find the right motif immediately. Not only do we complete the music swiftly, but Federico would even prefer that I didn't waste time jotting down what we've worked out. However, experience has taught him that I can totally forget a theme as fast as I've found it. Now he has me write it down on the spot. He insists, but never enough. In fact, the character in *The Clowns* whom I most identified with was the script girl, who never finds the notes she's made; she always loses them or forgets them.

QUESTION: Federico never goes to concerts, he never listens to records, he hates radios and jukeboxes, he can't even tolerate street musicians in restaurants, he always gets rid of them with a generous tip so long as they get lost. How do you explain this allergy of Fellini's to music?

ROTA: It's true, Federico flaunts his alienation to music, he's even coquettish about that, and I must admit I'm greatly flattered that he's come to all my works. I believe, however, that for Federico, it's really a form of self-defense, a protective measure. He can't listen to a single note without participating utterly. Music is never an accessory for him, it never complements the sounds in an environment. Federico isolates any music as a musical fact, and that's why he's caught by it, he falls victim to the musical emotion to which he cannot always afford to yield. That's why he constantly and doggedly rejects any type of music not strictly tied to his work. I've often noticed, for instance, that when a musical idea moves him, then even when he's heard it two thousand times, he'll still be moved at each hearing and with the same intensity. This means that Federico hears music deeply, that he feels it deeply, with force and precision. Not only that, but his capacity for not growing indifferent to a theme he's heard ad infinitum permits us to polish a motif carefully without getting sick of it. Because I'm also resistant to repetitions, which are actually indispensable.

24

The Gang

A FILM IMITATES and reproduces life more during its making than in its final state. That's why Fellini is so much at ease when guiding that incongruent apparatus, in the midst of that game of similarities, reflections, suggestions, needs, and vital questions. It's the only way he can work. You just couldn't imagine Fellini conceiving or writing a movie when locked up all alone in a room. Rome is not only a perfect place to live, it's the ideal city for a man who uses his own and other people's lives — life in its most immediate and spontaneous, most incredible and eternal expressions — as material for fantastic artistic speculations. For that reason, Rome is a kind of protective lair for Fellini, a perilous and attractive jungle, the familiar and unknown homeland, among whose landscapes and inhabitants he runs after discoveries, revelations, meanings.

Nor could you imagine Fellini shooting a film in an orderly, discreet, and silent atmosphere. To live, he needs an urgent and inexhaustible alternation of various realities and commitments. Likewise, to work, he draws the necessary concentration and tension from the teeming and chaotic presence of provisional and minor tensions and concentrations. In his work too, solitude is never a physical condition for him, a premise in the literal sense.

It almost seems like witchcraft — Fellini's ability to transform a group of people differing in their tasks and temperaments, to transmute them into a compact, effective unity, fully alive to achieving a common goal.

In fact, his capacity is the overall expression of two things. On the one hand, Fellini's personality — a potent concentrate of fascination, psychological intelligence, acting, vitality. And on the other hand, the unending, unflinching alert exercise of that personality, which joins a stable consciousness to a natural superiority. One has to observe Fellini for a long time to note distraction, weariness, between a mode of living and its practice, for the two are fused so harmoniously. It would be hard finding such unexhausted, always present lucidity. For it's not the programmatic adoption of a behavior foreign to Fellini's nature. It's really the conscious exaltation of an absolutely authentic nature.

Fellini's tireless irony, whether harsh or tender, and his penchant for making every situation and every person funny or grotesque allow him to reach into reality. And this vital, ever-active intervention is irreversible because Fellini neutralizes anyone else's ironical or critical judgment of him, rendering it useless and pointless with his sincere and skillful self-irony and self-criticism.

His kindness, his arrogant appeal, virtually his joyous physiological gratitude toward others, his astuteness, generosity, cruelty — in short, the extraordinary weight of Fellini's humanity — are a second mortgage put upon the outer world.

His impassiveness, his cordial but unfailing reserve about his own intimacy, his personal feelings, and emotions remove Fellini from any kind of real confidence and hence any obligating complicity with others.

Occasionally, someone tries to figure out the exact percentage

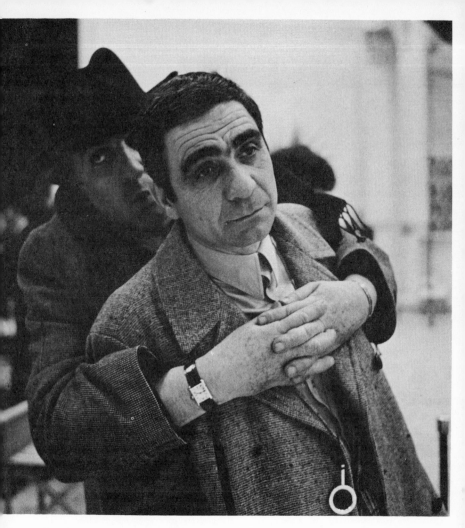

ellini with cameraman Giuseppe Rotunno

Fellini with Liliana Betti and scriptgirl Norma Giacchero

Liliana Betti and Norma Giacchero, drawn by Fellini

On the set with Nino Rota and (far right) Ettore Bevilacqua

On the set with writer Bernardino Zapponi

Assistant director Gerald Morin (left) with Danilo Donati, drawn by Fellini on the back of a menu

of Fellini's authorship in a film. The attempt is made with the unsuitable impartiality of mathematical operations or with the arbitrariness of personal convictions. The whole business is so absurd that it's not worth talking about even if the collective nature of the cinema would appear to justify it.

The making of a Fellini film is not so vastly different from that of other movies. It is not the bizarre result of a professional commitment like that of surgeons, astronauts, or magicians. Nor does Fellini ever write the script from start to finish, or draw the plan of a setting, or put up and switch on the lights, or inscribe the background motifs on the five-line stave.

And yet it seems as if he really did do all those things.

If I've intimated that Fellini's collaborators merely carry out what he wants, then I've done them a grave disservice and given him the futile lavishness of a saintly legend. Fellini could not possibly make his films with the help of indolent yes-men. Furthermore, those films, by their very nature, by their demands, by their prefigured existence, could not tolerate inadequate dedication or mediocre commitment. The originality of a motion picture consists in utilizing the individual contributions that go into it. And the process is not reversible. The value of these individual contributions will never reach the original value of the artwork.

In sum, the making of a Fellini film could be likened to a heist by a gang of criminals. And that is often the secret conviction of many producers.

25

The Assistant

Unreal as my secretarial job may have been, I had to take my function as an assistant director very literally and rigorously. Reality turned it into a kind of allegorical presence. In fact, I limited myself to attending the shootings of a Fellini film — and I was amazed, fascinated, or distracted. My inability to turn my "observation" status into concrete activity completely disoriented my convictions about and possible attitudes toward motion pictures.

It's true that I've worked only with Fellini. But contrary to what many people claim, that doesn't mean that my experience is with something unrelated to cinema. Quite the opposite. Fellini's cinema has the most authentic nature of this form of spectacle, its most exemplary expression, its qualitative and quantitative expansion. No one would go so far as to say, for instance, that a thinker's thought is more "thought" than that of a businessman, who thinks in his own way.

On the set, Fellini reminds me of man who, almost in a state of trance, is intent on executing the lines and figures of a drawing that he has already worked out in his mind.

His rapidity, certainty, and spontaneity in deciding upon frame after frame seem dictated by the invisible preexistence of these frames, which he alone can decipher in advance.

His freedom from any cinematic syntax is that of a man thoroughly familiar with the full topography of the story and moving about in it all the time and in every way without qualms or doubts. It's only when entering a new setting with the camera that Fellini shows the slight hesitation of a reader who, after going back over a chapter, stops for an instant and then immediately recognizes the nuances and the meaning.

Fellini's famous penchant for improvising, his natural way of adding, changing, omitting entire sequences or just individual scenes, has nothing to do with ex tempore moods, ideas, inspirations. Quite the contrary. It is the sole expression, the only indication of the unified creative tension that steers and modifies the film from the intuition that revealed it until its ultimate completion. Of course, the perspectives of an imagined drawing can never be as precise and immutable as a real composition. Imagination, which originally evoked them, tries to imprison them in its enigmatic transparency and polydimensionality, like certain dreams that follow one another and can be reconstructed in bits and pieces.

Fellini seems practically alone on the set when he composes a frame. Whether he's situating an actor or an object, putting a pleat in a dress or tousling someone's hair, he generally does it himself. At such times, he's often reminded me of those photographers forty years back, those frantic and hard-to-please men who, before taking a picture, stuck their heads out innumerable times from the black cloth and caracoled over to the customer in order to adjust his profile or push away a lamp or change the backdrop. Each single intervention in the scene is followed by a long, absorbed verification with the camera. And Fellini then looks like a scientist bent over his microscope, peering intently at the crystallizing process of disparate and indistinct substances until they rigorously, systematically, and inevitably reach their ultimate state of crystallization.

26

Forward with the Ocean

O**N THE SET**, Fellini becomes inexplicably patient — which helps him endure the endless waiting while a scene is prepared and lit. Not only that, but his patience can be irritatingly benevolent. It's the same kind of patience that he musters in general and that sometimes becomes a marvelous tolerance in difficult or unpleasant situations, delays, slow developments.

Yet, on the set, Fellini can also fall prey to an overwhelming impatience.

Whether he asks for the megaphone, the costume designer, or an unplanned wig, he never assumes that the megaphone may be fifty feet away (not unusual), the designer in the tailoring workshop, and the wig in the makeup department. Whatever he wants has to be there instantly. Otherwise he'll ask again a second later. And after another split second, he'll start demanding, more and more irritated. At such times, it is not only useless but perhaps quite hazardous to try placating him with sensible reasons or an appeal to the laws of time and space. If he simply limited himself to a curt retort, that would still prove his human irrationality. But no. He indulges his irritation in a tangle of incredible and sarcastic rebuttals, in abstract objections that ultimately sound as imperturbable as abstruse Taoist fiats.

An assistant informs him with the clearest conscience in the world that the actor picked for a certain role has been dead for two years. Fellini will answer impassively: "I don't care. I want him just the same. That's your problem."

Fellini never has the slightest doubts that anyone and anything participating in his movie — animal, vegetable, or mineral — must clairvoyantly know everything he, she, or it is supposed to do and achieve. "Why doesn't that peacock go to its assigned position?!" That's no longer a demand made on fantastic, omniscient animals. It's a human absurdity.

Practically every Fellini film has a sequence requiring fog. Getting that particular meteorological condition artificially (for Fellini, fog must signify a metaphysical "recurrence") is a delicate and difficult operation because it has to be computed to the right moment. Not too far and not too close to the sound of the clapstick. In filmmaking, there's no possible way of foreseeing the "right moment." It's a valid temporal concept only retrospectively. In fog scenes, Fellini's impatience runneth over. It explodes in a bacchanale of orders, indications, shouts, four-letter words, imprecations: "Fog! Fog! What about the fog?! What the fuck have you done with the fog? Stop that asshole over there, it's too much! Hey you, in that corner, keep pumping! Just look at that asshole! He's making fog behind the backdrop! Fog here! Fog there! That's enough fog! More fog! That fucking fog!"

Well, we have to realize that this avalanche of orders and insults causes even more confusion because it vanishes in the deafening roar of the fog machines. Voices and noise add to the chaos of the invisibility surrounding everyone, the dense cloud mass, in which the fog experts keep appearing and disappearing with their detonatorlike instruments, which make them look like furtive saboteurs.

For some time now, Fellini has tended to reconstruct not only settings but also natural elements that would seem impossible in a studio: the sea, for instance. While an army of stagehands was rhythmically moving an immense stretch of transparent plastic up and down, the studio was filled with the angry commands of a wretched Creation of the World: "Forward with the ocean! Away with the rain!"

If an actor makes the mistake of not instantly understanding what Fellini wants from him (a highly forgivable mistake since the actors are all amateurs), then the director's impatience turns into cruelty. Even an actor's deafness isn't an acceptable excuse for Fellini. On the contrary, it's downright fraudulent. His exasperation at such a time even interferes with the lucid exposition of what he wants. So the actor gets more and more bewildered, merely increasing Fellini's irritation, which, in a kind of irreparable and delirious counterpoint, makes the actor more and more disoriented. At various times, such situations can have fateful epilogues: a brawl, a fistfight, a gunshot. On the other hand . . .

27

Dario and Bario

No one suspected it could happen.

Yet the premises were all there and quite perfect at that. The very background smelled of predestination. The film was *The Clowns,* and the scene was a memorial to two great clowns of the past: Dario and Bario. The direct cause promptly showed that any trust in the banal solution of miracles is incurable: Two men — I won't say actors, because they weren't — were asked to stand in front of the camera and speak lines they didn't know by characters they didn't know either. The second condition aggravated the matter in its own way: for diverse reasons, the two men were both incapable of reciting lines.

The first man was an obscure extra, who looked like a primitive and solitary shepherd: a hooked nose, two placid, sheeplike eyes. There were rumors that the shepherd managed to rake in his few thousand lire thanks to a convention that is widespread in the cinema: the privilege of having a sickness in the family. Supposedly, the shepherd had a daughter who'd been hospitalized for a long time. But this was never confirmed. For one thing, did the little girl truly exist? And if she did exist, was she really ill? Or else — a hypothesis that made the blood run cold — was the poor thing as healthy as a fish but deliberately kept prisoner in a hospital to justify the father's atrocious privilege?

The second performer was an excellent Swiss mime, whose unusual gift apparently could be explained through a specific defect: he was a deaf-mute.

The third factor closing the series with malign consistency was: an entry of the clowns entitled *The Declaration* and based on a reiteration mechanism that can become perilously disorienting.

The man behind it all, i.e., the director of *The Clowns*, unwittingly responsible for all three factors, was unequivocally Fellini. He was accustomed to ignoring the fact that you can't speak lines you don't know. He had cast the shepherd and the deaf-mute and decided upon the entrance of the clowns. Secretly planning to outdo himself that day in foresight and scheduling, the director automatically waved off all responsibility for the three factors the instant he became aware of them. His was a childish reaction to a sense of guilt, which in other people can arouse a suicidal or schizophrenic mea culpa.

Was the situation disastrous? that was the fault of the situation. The overture was bad enough, even though it barely hinted at what followed. The mime had hardly spent two minutes looking at the only available script of *The Declaration*, while the shepherd sat in a corner, waiting for his turn to read. He was calm and secure, as though he had already done a brilliant job of everything. Fellini pounced upon them, tore the script from the mime's hands, and began reading both their lines, shouting them out haphazardly, dragging the two clowns convulsively this way and that way, pushing them together, pulling them apart, knocking them together again. He was in the throes of a horrible, delirious, irrational mood, while the clowns let him have his way, bewildered and docile. In their

Fellini during the filming of *The Clowns*

Fellini with assistants Liliana Betti and Maurizio Mein (right) visiting circus director Nando Orfei (second from left)

White clown, drawn by Fellini

Fellini with Victoria Chaplin in *The Clowns*

amazement, they quite justifiably couldn't understand what Fellini wanted of them. The rehearsal was a failure, and so the shepherd and the mime were dragged into the circus ring and abandoned in front of the camera like deserters before a firing squad.

The shepherd was supposed to play Dario, the white clown: elegant, authoritarian, astute, violent, logical, hysterical. This casting seemed incredible, a mistake. But only by conventional reasoning. The erect cluster of hair on the head, the face rigid with white make-up, the hooked nose, and placid gaze with its aggressive awareness, the shiny, black-satin costume reaching down to the calves, the translucent white stockings under the vast overalls, the effeminate black patent-leather dancing slippers — all these things gave the crude shepherd a metaphysical goatlike elegance, that terrifying mixture of shininess, sharpness, and devilishness (a strange, lithe centaur) typical of the white clown.

The Swiss mime was Bario, and he felt very much at ease in the dizzy role of August because it concealed him, protected him from the chaotic situation.

Since it was obvious that the declaration of love would drag on and on in these conditions, Fellini decided to lose no time. He quickly formed a circle of three. Off-camera, he spoke and mimed Dario's lines. In front of him, on camera, the real Dario was implored to imitate Fellini's gestures passively and repeat the lines that Bario in turn had to repeat to the linen mannequin in woman's clothing. The simple scheme promptly revealed an unfortunate hitch. There was no doubt that the shepherd could concentrate on only one thing at a time. He imitated Fellini's gestures (and with a bombast that could be called somewhat ironic), but he didn't quite get the lines. He mutilated them, they became inconsistent and thus even more incomprehensible to the poor mime, who could only lip-read and hence deformed them totally, pronouncing the words in his hesitant, choking way.

The shepherd's obtuseness and the mime's deafness were countered by Fellini's brutal and raging impatience, which passed from insult to threat, from sarcasm to hysterical attack, and ultimately to self-incrimination. The only result was to aggravate the obtuseness and the deafness, arousing the shepherd's bored and petulant vexation and increasing the mime's confusion and mortification. Fellini forgot that his own fury could easily make him irreparably bewildered as a result of some epilogue to that crazy pantomime. In fact, without his control, which had the effect of violence, everybody would have totally lost his bearings in that mad jungle of echoes, refrains, and repetitions, which seemed to calm down only in more and more insane, more and more surprising divagations. Thus, the shepherd recited: "Signorina, the moment I saw you, I stopped living!" And he put his hand on his chest, the right side, for the irrefutable reason — which he confessed with self-complaisant modesty — that *his* heart was on the right.

It did no good telling Fellini that the mime was a deaf-mute. As though the defect were the mime's fault, Fellini replied with laconic fury: "I know! I know!" But not even a subsequent calm and detachment could render him more objective. If anyone told him that it was impossible to ask Catomi (the shepherd) for more mental elasticity, that it was as absurd and ruthless as demanding the acting skill of a Laurence Olivier from, say, a coal miner, Fellini would retort with an almost suitable paradox: "But Catomi isn't the miner. *He's the coal!!*" And the director's viewpoint wasn't at all hampered by the fact tht he himself had picked the coal. If he had made his choice in order to achieve a lifelike depiction of Dario through its very reverse, Catomi's absolute implausibility, then he also had to accept any risks in that tricky undertaking.

Finally, it happened: something that no one would ever have suspected. A famous clown entrance was enriched by a new and extraordinary figure — an all the more valuable version, which we can only hope will remain unchanged. And the classic substance — both comical and reactionary — of all clown entrances had acquired an important addition.

28

Whither, Fortune?

FELLINI'S CRUELTY toward a bewildered actor can be so
frankly violent as to reach heights of comical cynicism. There
was once a poor woman, a woeful accordionist, devoured by
that gloomy misery that inevitably becomes a tortured sense of
persecution. For months and months, she harassed Fellini with
utterly desperate letters, with mute and dramatic appearances
on the threshold of his offices, with musical performances whose
depths of sadness were accompanied by the heartrending woe of
the accordion, the intimidating words of the song "Whither,
Fortune?," and, last but certainly not least, her tears. With that
unforeseeable and absurd patience of his, Fellini put up with
the torment for several months.

One day, he called the accordionist in because he wanted her
to play herself in a documentary he was making for American
television. The poor woman was stunned by an event that so

abruptly smashed the unbroken chain of her ill luck. She was paralyzed by the fear of making mistakes or by an unconscious desire to make them so as keep her desolate situation intact. As a result, once she was on the set, she lost any capacity for acting or performing. All she could offer the camera was an obstinate and furious impassiveness. No self-laceration, no agitation, no outbursts of weeping, no "Whither, Fortune?"

Fellini did everything in his power to break open some aperture in that tense stubbornness. He tried sweetness, harshness, persuasion. Finally, he walked up to her and shouted in her ear, shouted these monstrously reasonable words: "Don't you see how miserable you are? Even now you're having horrible luck!" The instinct of self-preservation has automatic laws. All at once, the accordionist popped out of her grayish, suicidal inertia and went back to her normal, dismal liveliness. As Fellini wanted her to do. But his effective cynicism cost him dearly. For further, long-lasting months, he had to put up with her doleful persecution. Atrociously pigheaded, she kept following him and asking for comfort and reassurance as to the quality of her performance on that day.

It's a rare amateur actor who can speak his lines promptly and correctly. He's nearly always distracted by the effort of recalling the words and pronouncing them with the proper inflections. He may therefore even forget to do the gestures and movements — far more important to Fellini — or else perform them unevenly, hesitatingly.

To surmount any obstacles that could waste a good deal of time, Fellini has come up with the "number system" or "numerological diction." Instead of lines, the actor has to count off numbers in their normal order. For instance, a line of fifteen words equals an enumeration up to thirty. The actor merely counts till thirty: 1-2-3-4-5-6-7, etc. In this way, Fellini has a much easier time directing the actor without perturbing him: Take three steps forward. Turn your head to the left. Smile. Raise your head. Now look right. Stroke your hair. Now sigh. Keep walking. Now stop. Just stand there motionless.

Hence, one can rather frequently catch squabbles like this:
Fellini: "Why didn't you raise your head at nine?"

Actress: "I *did* raise my head at nine!"

Fellini: "That's not true. You raised your head at twelve."

Actress: "No, at nine!"

Fellini: "Well, then count faster!"

It seems impossible that an actor maneuvered like an object can appear lifelike and effective on the screen. And yet it's precisely the cold geometry of gestures and actions decided externally, the absence of any conscious participation by the actor, that lends such acute presence to the characters in a Fellini film.

Often, Fellini puts off casting a part until the last moment, and it doesn't matter whether the actor is lay or professional. Once, early in the morning, a piano tuner with a bashful, good-natured Mickey Mouse face was grabbed on his threshold, thrust into a car, driven off to Cinecittà, squeezed into a tuxedo, put on the set, and told to count up to sixty. All that within thirty minutes. The poor man could only sweat and count, sweat and count, with a terrorized expression on his face. Beyond forty, his counting speeded up, becoming frantic, as though he felt a machine gun nuzzling his spine. Shooting the sequence with the "kidnapped man" took something like a week. But after the second day, he moved about in the studio and on the roads of Cinecittà as securely and tranquilly as a veteran of the screen. Who could say — perhaps he had only dreamed he was a piano tuner? Now he absolutely didn't know who he was. But so what!

To stay in the field of music: sometimes an actor has risked a schizophrenic identification because Fellini was so arrogant and jokingly stubborn about rebuking the man for not being the character he was interpreting. The actor Barrocci, with his round, soft, hairless face and his big childlike eyes, was supposed to play a music teacher directing two little nuns on the piano. But the moment the playback began, his arms executed such wrong, clumsy, mechanical motions that they became utterly incomprehensible. And not even Fellini, with his wild imagination, could grasp them in order to stop them. The outcome? During the work pauses, Fellini walked over to Barrocci and asked him desolately: "Why in the world did you want to study music, Barrocci? . . . I don't understand where you got the idea of pursuing a vocation that isn't yours . . . hmmm!"

The first few times, the actor responded to the obstinate baiting by protesting in annoyance that he had never studied music, that he had never even dreamed of studying it.

But then, Fellini asked him for the umpteenth time: "Don't you too find it mysterious that you wanted to study music?" And Barrocci's big, perplexed face began to show the worried conviction that perhaps it really *was* mysterious. Perhaps it really *had* been a mistake.

For a long time, many ladies in the aristocracy or bourgeoisie or in the cultural and artistic jungle of the capital were intent on landing a bit part in a Fellini movie. This was apparently an indispensable experience of life for them, a social achievement, snobbery, a coveted cinematic disease like German measles. A few of them expected something utterly irrevocable.

A bad mood on the director's part, a moment of confusion, a misunderstood instruction, and Fellini was already thundering the noblewoman's name, twisting it in front of a hundred people, adding a terse invective:

"Lucifredda del Asshole!!!!!"

If, however, this terrible incident happened to Alessandra Mannoukine, it could have a graceful aftermath, much to Fellini's disadvantage. Alessandra Mannoukine is an adorable old character actress of Russian background, and she looks like a colored and sucked-down caramel. (In contrast, her husband, also an actor, looks like a licorice stick.) Alessandra has the cordial vacuousness of an empty box. Fellini wants her in every one of his movies, perhaps just to fight with her.

For over a quarter of an hour, Mannoukine had been arduously trying to think her way into her part. But all she managed to attain was the nebulous awareness of being in a studio.

Fellini, crimson with annoyance and about to resort to bloodshed, yelled out: "Mannoukine del Asshole!"

Alessandra, tranquil and stupefied (in her, stupor signifies extreme attention), asked in a solemn accent: "Vot means Asshole?"

The assistant director, at her side, realized that to get out of the impasse and continue work, it was necessary to come up with some kind of answer. Otherwise, Mannoukine would keep asking ad infinitum. Embarrassed and amused, he whispered some vague explanation to her. Alessandra, still tranquil and stupefied (the same stupor also signifies malaise), yelled at Fellini: "Please, to me you use nice vords!"

Mannoukine wasted another half hour before her tremendous and spastic mental efforts helped her to grasp what she had to do. But Fellini now acted as if everything was all right.

The intimacy between Fellini and the performer truly becomes an enchanted dialogue when the director, off camera, becomes a "support" for the actor or actress. Isolated in the harsh glare of the spotlights, eyes fixed on the objective, the performer smiles, asks, talks to the director, a dark silhouette in the penumbrous aura surrounding the set and therefore more overwhelming, more hypnotic. Fellini's head is tilted to the side, almost grazing the camera. His eyes squint to take in the space of the frame. And he displays the behavior typical for him at such times: the eagerness and crafty satisfaction of the satyr, who peers out at his victim, indicating her movements as though to relish them or suggest them to her. Then, to better ensnare the victim, he embodies any character whatsoever, miming the body language and imitating the voice. The darkness, in which Fellini's mimetic liveliness dissolves, has mysterious, alarming echoes for the actor, as though he were drawn to indistinct mirages, inveigled by sudden metamorphoses.

Often, these dialogues take humorous turns. For with penetrating exactness, Fellini can, indifferently, play the part of a nasty little girl, a drunk, a lover swooning into orgasm, a fop, a nymphomaniac, a priest, a lady manager. On such occasions, Fellini proves what a marvelous actor he can be. But at the same time, certain things confirm that he could never have become an actor: the imperceptible irony corroding the character and the brilliant acting skill that makes him exasperate the character, poke subtle and malicious fun at him, thereby declaring his own natural inability fully to identify with him.

Apart from the protagonists with whom the director experiences a highly singular and complex rapport (as I have already emphasized), the remaining actors know little or nothing — not so much about the film, but about the characters they are playing. That little bit is picked up from a stray page or two of their lines or from their costumes (the least certain signs). That nothing — an ineffable nothing — comes from the "number system." They would never take the chance of asking Fellini for clarification. If they did, they would get nothing but benevolent irony or even more frustrating secrecy. And asking the assistants or anyone else would be mortifying. So they have to wait for the film's release and go to see it if they want to find out who they are.

Meanwhile, during the shooting, their maximum effort goes into dignified concealment of their malaise, anxiety, and embarrassment. And they mange this with exaggerated nonchalance that the confusion in the studio permits.

Some, the ones least familiar with the milieu, run around, lost, their faces covered with some kind of suffering. Or else they are lay actors, who, by having to count, are even more at sea about their parts. They follow the shooting of the various frames with a rapt, greedy attention that would deserve very different goals, as they try to reconstruct the ever-elusive reason for their presence in this place. Or else they pretend that they just happen to be walking along past Fellini and the set designer, who are standing there, conversing. Or else they halt next to them, peering left and right as though looking for some person or object to move toward. All this just to catch a stray word, a half sentence that could enlighten them. They don't even know about what anymore. So long as they're enlightened.

29

The PR Office

I WAS DETERMINED to flee any further experience on the set as an assistant director, and I was convinced that the PR office was a more autonomous film sector because it was more peripheral. My desire to escape was so stubborn and agitated, my illusion was so firm and overemphatic, that I neglected a rather blatant fact that would have discouraged anyone else: the PR office for the new movie didn't exist. Or at least, it wouldn't exist during the first few months of work.

Very patient, Fellini eventually fulfilled my wishes. His only comment was: "Do you really think it's more interesting and entertaining to talk on the phone with a man from a daily or weekly paper than to an actor like Chiodo or a bit player like Capitani?" Saintly words.

The truth is that it was almost impossible to talk about *Roma*. It was no coincidence that Fellini had always refused to discuss

rt Lancaster visiting the studio

iana Betti with Anouk Aimée and Albert Finney

Lunch with Louis Malle

Sergio Leone visits the studio

the film at length. He must have sensed and then confirmed the vast difference that ultimately developed between what he was doing and what he managed to say about it. And besides, what the director says is almost never connected to the film itself. It's really more about the intimate, private relationship that he needs to have with the movie in order to make it. During the preparations, the film had already discouraged or destroyed any sort of mediation between itself and the public. I believe that with *Roma* Fellini went to the extreme of the kind of cinema he has been pursuing for many years: the kind in which the image becomes the absolute experience of reality. At this point, the image relates to experience like a menu to the dishes that it lists.

For this reason, the PR office for *Roma* quickly turned out to be a mere distributor of the film's menu: Rome in childhood memories — the arrival in Rome — Raccordo Anulare — Villa Borghese — the Barafonda Theater — the subway — the brothels — the ecclesiastical fashion show — Trastevere. As indicated more by the titles than the episodes (the latter term might improperly suggest a narrative), the film was about places and moments. Nor was it possible to add anything to the mere names, for the film was made up exclusively of those places and moments. It completely materialized their essence as indicated by the names.

One thing was certain. After *La Dolce Vita* and *Satyricon*, this was the third film that Fellini dedicated to Rome. Despite the varying uses of the city in each movie, I believe that the motive was always identical. Perhaps Fellini has the same visceral relationship to Rome as a scientist has to his guinea pigs. And just as the scientist is grateful to his guinea pigs for allowing him to perform his experiments, so too Fellini loves this city and returns to it. For it is only by living among its familiar perspectives or simply adopting its material that he can bear his increasingly lucid and pitiless testimony to our age.

Now just what was *Roma* beyond the city that was its protagonist? I recall that every time I came to the set during the shooting, I was struck by one detail. The settings and periods could change, but the spectacle before the camera was always the same: human beings condemned to live through their empty fetishes, old or new, in perpetual motion. The ferocious spectators in the small Barafonda Theater and the dismal heroes of variety acts on stage. The grim parades of the Fascists and their cringing public. The lugubrious and festive ecclesiastical fashion show and its onlookers, pale, mournful masks. The insane ringaround of the prostitutes before ravenous clients. The absurd carousel of traffic on Raccordo Anulare. The trip into the huge technological belly of a subway during its construction. The giddy swarming of a crowd celebrating in Trastevere as in a dark infernal aquarium. And last but not least, the silly, noisy excursion through the nocturnal city by some thirty young centaurs, the sterile representatives of an obscurantist or decadent rebellion. Never had Fellini so exalted the individual by celebrating the lowly rites of the collectivity.

But all that was already an interpretation, and certainly a highly precarious one. Whereas we know that the explicit job of a PR office is information. Unfortunately, with *Roma*, the information always inevitably turned into the schematic method of the menu.

Meanwhile, Fellini, completely absorbed in his work, was adamant in his refusal to give interviews, see journalists, or speak about the film. The journalists, however, were equally implacable in their siege. They kept calling and calling to ask for interviews, to talk to Fellini, and to find out about the film. With the zeal of a rug dealer or the breathless impertinence of certain peddlers who station themselves near famous sanctuaries, I tried to elude the persistence of the journalists by indiscriminately offering them stills from the movie, old résumés on the director, ten mimeographed pages from the scenario of *Roma*, and various bulletins that I was gradually compiling on each sequence. No way! In most cases, the attempts, which could go on for weeks and weeks, systematically concluded with an explicit: "Either Fellini or nothing!" All that led me to conclude that the PR office for a Fellini movie begins and ends with Fellini himself.

The matter had its risks. But also its advantages. The few journalists who resigned themselves to a secondhand Fellini

Anna Magnani with her dogs, drawn by Fellini

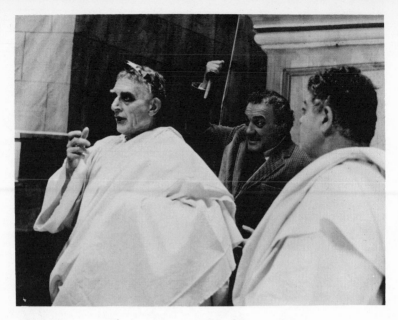

The assassination of Julius Caesar. Fellini directing *Roma*

The fashion show of the prelates

e teacher's protest

The Noantri festa

The Teatrino della Barafonda

The fashion show of the prelates

The Noantri festa

Roma, the young man in the luxury brothel

were generally sent by provincial newspapers or foreign magazines and film journals, usually in South America or in the East.
They came into the office, took their swollen envelope of photographic and historical material on the movie, and vanished. We
would exchange friendly greetings, but not another word. And
what could we have said? Yet the Fellini interviews that these
pariahs of the PR office had to invent were frequently more authentic (aside from a faint anemia for lack of real experience)
than the ones that were the privileges of newspapers with large
circulations.

In regard to these true interviews, *Roma* had an almost total
catastrophe. However, the castastrophe was in part contained
because Fellini gave very few interviews, perhaps only four or
five at the most. Still, these few sufficed to establish an unprec-
edented casuistry. Some of them dissolved in thin air, and we
never heard anything more about the interviews or the writers,
who then vanished God knows where, perhaps into a mercenary
army in Africa. As for the other interviews, they were — to put
it mildly — unbelievable. The journalist, almost always sent by
some huge weekly, would meet Fellini. The two men would
lunch together, and between courses the director would chat
extensively about the film. After which, the interviewer was invited to the set to watch some takes. So far, so good. But a week
later, the magazine editor would call, and, as if it were the most
natural thing in the world, request a second interview, as
though several months had passed and Fellini were about to
make another film. We never found out what it was that mo-
tivated the need for a second interview. Perhaps upon trying to
coordinate his notes on Fellini's fascinating but, by their very
nature, chaotic meanderings, the newspaperman had been unable to find his bearings and had ultimately foundered. Or else,
if he did achieve something, the result may have left him rather
perplexed. At any rate, the magazine editor sent out a second
man, who already knew Fellini, so that the greater familiarity
might avert another failure. But in point of fact, the expedient
only served to stave off disaster; it did not really solve anything.
On the contrary. The second interviewer, Fellini's "friend,"
confronted the director more nonchalantly and decisively. He

listened with an attention that was protected by dangerous old
convictions. In the end, his article used the same language, the
same viewpoints, even the same anecdotes as some older
reportage on *La Dolce Vita*.

Interviewing Fellini is relatively simple, once you manage to
get around his adamancy. All you have to do is, say, wander
through the studio and patiently wait for a free moment between takes. At this point, the director–journalist encounter is a
sure thing. Fellini so greatly identifies with the film he is making that anyone coming into contact with the film, even by his
sheer presence on the set, automatically communicates with
Fellini.

The difficulties begin when the interviewer has to put down
the interview, record it in black and white. At this moment, he
realizes it was no use catching everything on tape, writing scrupulous notes in his pad. Once the material is separated from its
author, a peculiar degeneration turns it into something else,
often inferior to the original. The key to a Fellini interview is
indisputably Fellini himself. The answers he gives, the opinions
he formulates, the stories he tells, preserve their meaning and
authenticity only if they can survive in their original context.
And this context is made up of: a tireless penchant for deforming and expanding everything, an aggressive and provocative
sense of humor, an only seeming availability, at bottom a misleading game of mirrors that protects an inner reserve, a taste
for destructive paradox, a pleasure in sensational yet always sig-
nificant contradiction, in unexpected yet — in its own way —
illuminating retraction, in a surprising yet revealing conclusion.

Usually, however, when the interview is being set down, this
phase omits either of the two aspects of a Fellini interview: the
content and the expression. The outcome is almost always an in-
sipid mutilation. Either it's a presentation of a stereotype character who has been portrayed for decades with the same quirks,
the same coyness, the same gestural and psychological reper-
toire — a presentation larded with summarized answers, fragments of statements, or simply isolated and thus incomprehensible lines. Or else there's an inert sequence of questions and

answers, faithfully reported but torn from any context and severed from the person, so that they lose some of their tang, which is also their meaning.

No one can reasonably deny that an interview is a very simple journalistic convention, one of the most frequent and elementary formulas used by the mass media. Assuming, however, that the two determinants, i.e., the interviewer and the interviewee, rigorously adhere to their roles. The interviewer has to inquire as precisely, directly, and impersonally as he can. The interviewee, on the other hand, has to codify his own personality (whether or not it's his real one doesn't matter) and every nexus and connection — outlooks on life, tastes, preferences, choices, work, projects and their motives, results and their meanings, etc., etc. — in answers that are as exhaustive and definitive as possible.

With Fellini, this rigid schema quickly falls apart. And quite loudly. The cold, abstract convention, its anonymous terms, its fixed roles — everything gets confused and discolored in the simple, intense, and always hazardous encounter of two human beings who meet with curiosity, sympathy, spontaneity, who, albeit for the paltry commitment of the occasion, are striving for mutual discovery and for modest and ephemeral clarification of the themes that are brought up. The sense of humor, the bantering tone, the playful attitude that Fellini demonstrates in the human contact (as which he sees an interview) can have various goals. The first is to wipe out the silly pretentious gravity of the journalistic convention. The second is to preserve that timidity toward himself and that alert and impertinent lucidity and awareness that never abandon him. The third may be purely contingent, i.e., the attempt to somehow neutralize an exhilaratingly unsuitable question:

The journalist, sotto voce, in a confidential tone, after peering about suspiciously: "How do you imagine God?"

Fellini, appalled: "I'm amazed that you could still have doubts in that respect. . . . You have him before you!"

If the interlocutor is open and sensitive, he will limit himself to reporting factually on the encounter with the director. He will preserve the interview's effervescent, wraithlike, contradictory nature, the relaxed and provisional quality. His testimony, though not exhaustive, will at least be authentic; not definitive, but at least meaningful. If, however, the iron exigencies of the mass media gain the upper hand, then all the emotional, imaginative, intellectual material gathered during the encounter will slip through the deathly and all-knowing meshes of convention.

Things seem to go better if the newspaperman selects a more autonomous and suggestive route, i.e., an article, portrait, or feature written in the first person and following a discreet and simple observation of Fellini at work. But this greater ease is only ostensible. In reality, if the interviewer is not bewildered by the elusiveness of Fellini's concrete presence, then he, the interviewer, will have to resign himself merely to report on the more enigmatic, more unfathomable echoes, shadows, reflections of that more passive presence. So the interviewers who simply invent, who imagine Fellini, are better off. Their hypotheses will at least have the reasonable solidity of undisputed convictions.

And then, you never can tell. Does Fellini protest upon learning from a newspaper that he belongs to an organization for the advancement of Lapps, that he has joined a subcommittee of the Common Market, that he is an enthusiastic member of a nudist club? Is Fellini surprised to receive an anxious letter from the artistic director of the Paris Opera, asking him where to locate a squad of midgets? No. But why not?

30

Amarcord

"WHAT ABOUT the mosquitoes? Is there going to be a mosquito invasion in the movie? I was talking about it to my sister last night, and we were wondering . . ."

Fellini: "But of course. The 1940 mosquito invasion of Agro Pontino. It'll be one of the most terrifying sequences! . . ."

"Thank you very much, Signor Fellini, and thank you on the part of my sister too. We were sure of it!"

This telephone call managed to pierce the barrier of the various switchboards and offices in Cinecittà. But it was worth it. Fellini's new film had been announced. Its title? *Invaded Man.* A dizzying avalanche of versions and hypotheses about the particular existential state of the anonymous protagonist was eagerly supplied by the director, propagated by the PR offices, or just spontaneously generated. No doubt, the most astonishing and audacious speculation was that telephone call. Its scientific façade, its documentary claim, its suggested invader — the mosquitoes — made it a sublime apologia, not for the coming film, of course, but for what a Fellini film can be: to Fellini himself, to others, to everybody.

And the apologia enchanted me. Once again, disgracefully. I had decided to give *Amarcord* my professional commitment, almost intolerant of the climate, the special atmosphere around and within any Fellini film. This atmosphere is dense with unusual things, surprising factors, inconceivable characters, madness, diziness, vitality, a seething and tormenting life. But my efforts were useless. It's like claiming to breathe air and not the oxygen in the air. The mosquitoes were enough to make me throw in the sponge. In this umpteenth and ignominious relapse into curiosity and participation, the only possible and at all dignified resistance was to make simple notes, jottings, very private memos, that scarcely restrained the motives behind them. And now, the only possible and at all decent revenge for my abject recidivism is to make notes and jottings like these, wild and disorderly. But perhaps it's a false revenge. Who knows? Perhaps only immediacy, faithfulness, a broken description, could manage, however vaguely, to reproduce the feverish adventure of working on a Fellini film — reproduce it without bogging down in anecdotes.

Emilia, the Marches, Lombardy; Cesena, Forlimpopoli, Rimini, Lugo di Romagna, Pesaro, Milan. Plenary meetings of amateur cinema societies, public appeals to all and sundry. Fellini travels, sees, evaluates, takes notes, has hundreds of types photographed, summons dozens of them to Rome. Repeatedly. Enough to populate an entire little town.

But inevitably, as usual, the express train from Naples pours them into the film: high-school teachers, Fascists, shopkeepers, fathers for Titta, mothers for Titta, grandfathers for Titta, Biscein. And even Giudizio. It doesn't matter whether he lives in Rome.

Fellini wanted to see a woman to consider her for the part of Titta's mother.

Bruno Zanin as Titta in *Amarcord* (right)

Fellini at the tests for the class photograph

From left to right: Nando Orfei (Pataca), Pupella Maggio (Titta's mother), Armando Brancia (Titta's father), Bruno Zanin (Titta), and Stefano Proietti (Oliva)

Fellini filming *Amarcord*

"Have you ever been in a film, Signora?"

"No. Just occasionally on television in Naples. . . ."

"What did you do exactly?"

(After an embarrassing pause): "Well . . . I don't know . . . I showed human emotions. . . ."

A general or merely specific tendency: the script is quantitatively reduced for the final movie version. Numerous situations, moments, characters disappear. The film, on the contrary, tends to amplify each situation, enriching it with developments and presences. I don't know why all that reminds me of Fellini's reluctance to travel, move about, see new places.

Fellini's office. Auditions.

Fellini: "What's your favorite kind of part, Signora? Your forte?"

Signora: "None — I don't have a forte."

Fellini: "But you're an actress?"

Signora: "No I'm not."

Fellini: "But you were called in?"

Signora: "No. I wasn't called in."

Fellini: "Well, then you came on your own. Would you like to do something in the film?"

Signora: "No, I don't want to do anything in the film."

Fellini: "Well, then why did you come?"

Signora: "To see the show! To get to know the show!"

Fellini: "What show?"

Signora: "You, Signor Fellini! The Fellini show!"

Mother to her daughter: "Ah, now I can die. Now, I've met Fellini! Ah, I can get cancer now. I've seen Fellini!"

All the educational institutions of Rome and Latium had been sifted. But no Titta could be found. Understandably. My timidity made the search a kind of absurd rite. Skeptical and sprightly, with a funereal, aristocratic pallor, Nestor accompanied me on my visits to various schools. He entered the classrooms first, while I tried to hide behind him as long as pos-

sible. Often, I didn't even go in. And so Nestor, upon concluding the introductory talk, turned around to introduce a phantom
Signora Betti, assistant to Fellini. But she had assumed the arcane semblance of the school janitor behind him.

Among the principals, two or three, graceless or regretful,
vigorously refused to let us enter their institutions. They suspected us of being dangerous emissaries of some new subver-
sive power or other. Others, naïve and avuncular, received us
warmly, hoping to direct the anxiety-provoking disquiet of the
students toward less ferocious goals.

An employee of the tax office, with the dumbfounded look of
a kindly cutthroat. How can you tell him that he's going to play
a crazy uncle? The problem of not revealing to the candidates
the definitions of their characters, often inspired by physical
defects, psychological blemishes, pathological manias.

Screen test for a Volpina.
First Volpina: "Yes, fine, thank you! Certainly, thank you, Signor Fellini! Of course, of course, the little wolf, thank you, the
burning viscera, of course! I get it! Thank you. The blazing
womb, of course! Thank you, thank you, Signor Fellini! Dilated nostrils, of course, right away! Thank you!"

Fellini wants to thank all the people who tested but were
rejected for some part, even for objective reasons. His letters,
in a melancholy tone, softened by a friendly humor, are full of
gratitude and, even more, of explanations and reasons that are
so flattering and charming that the rejectees will have the comforting feeling of escaping a disaster, or at least brilliantly passing the most grueling examinations. In fact, each of them will
hear that he didn't get the part because he was (it all depends)
too: likable, intelligent, nice, witty, fascinating, sensitive, with
it, innocent, passionate, aware, intense, lucid, attractive, fresh,
dignified, etc., etc. To what extent does Fellini's cordiality
coexist with the demand of a landscape dreamed up by Bosch?
The important thing in this gigantic justification is not to mix up
the envelopes and addresses of those who have been "spared."

Otherwise, Nereo Rocco, the trainer of the Milan soccer team, could be told that he is not sufficiently catlike and ugly for the part of Volpina.

I return an unusable photo to Fellini: "The guy died two years ago!"

With his glasses perched on his nose, Fellini merely looks up and protests with impassive sweetness: "I don't care. He's exactly right for the part." Or else he doesn't protest at all. He merely slips the photo lovingly into one of his huge, perennially reviewed files. That too is a way of surviving.

Inside Cinecittà, the "small town" is emerging little by little. It's convincing and fragile, like certain modern constructions that can collapse suddenly or flake away slowly. Is even reality today becoming the mere representation of itself?

Biscein is the raggedy, starving braggart of the town. Giudizio, the town idiot. If madness and imagination happen to be the same thing, why not fuse the two characters into one? If Fellini doesn't think of such dizzying experiments, then the momentary actor does. The actor doing Biscein is Neapolitan, and his name is Ombra [shadow] (some names are such brilliant syntheses). His face is indescribable because it combines elements that have no apparent motives for being together. Fellini says he looks like the blow-up of a bacteria — and I add: a winking and joking bacteria. In front of the camera, Ombra plunges into the classic catastrophe: uncontrolled movements, forgetfulness, unbelievable initiatives, and an unbridled obstinacy in repeating a mistake more and more tidily and efficiently. Fellini, for his part, has the classic raptus of impatience, rage, sudden tenderness, shouting, imploring, Attila-like threats, crushing remarks, amorous sweetness. Secure and untouchable, Obra tries to justify himself — to others and to himself. But not even the clairvoyant sensitivity of a great performer could make his explanations credible: "I'm allergic to wool! This is wool! The sandpaper you used to make the wool look old — I can feel it down my spine. It's maddening!" Or else he indulges in eager but incomprehensible technical reflections: "Of course, filming with eight-kilometer film is a different matter! I'm used to eight-millimeter film! Here a pile of film is being wasted on me, and film costs a lot of money!" What was he in a past life: a potter, a lathe, a revolution counter?

The scene being shot is one of Biscein's lies. Biscein enters a Grand Hotel suite housing some thirty concubines in an emir's harem. He takes out a pipe and begins to play, while the women, swathed in veils, abandon themselves in an increasingly frenetic belly dance. The metaphor is the transparent allusion to a huge embrace, an overwhelming sexual exploit. The thirty concubines are thus dancing for Biscein. But Fellini, scarcely off camera, is mortifying Biscein in front of them, attacking him, teasing him. No liar was ever so clamorously exposed and with such cruel simultaneity.

If you lightly scratch the surface of a Fellini actor, you'll find the character for which he's been chosen. Ombra is really Biscein. For instance, he says he's a magazine publisher. It goes without saying that publishing is an activity that viscerally, telepathically links all the people involved in it. Today, as a matter of fact, Giulio Einaudi is coming to the set. Is he here to discuss a publishing project with Fellini or to comfort his colleague Ombra? When coincidences multiply, they give you pause to think. Einaudi is accompanied by a famous English feminist, who unexpectedly sees the sparkling harem scene, the most abject expression of the mortification of women. Well, every woman has the publisher she deserves.

Elisabetta, a character actress, says to Fellini: "What a head, you have, Doc. What a head you have!"

Fellini: "I understand, but what do you want?"

Elisabetta (impatiently): "What's your head size, Doc? I'd love to knit you a woolen stocking-cap, a stocking-cap with white and pink stripes. . . ."

Talking about *Amarcord* or writing about it is a disheartening enterprise; it can make you feel utterly dejected. The situations, gestures, characters are such usual and at the same time such splendidly objectified examples that one is constantly torn between the frustration of listing them anonymously or the even more frustrating temptation somehow to render their effectiveness, their savor. Or else the continual torment of describing the clothes, the things, the objects. Fellini has virtually miniaturized the story. Aside from the situations, he narrates a gesture, an article of apparel, an object.

The teachers.

Fides is a lady from Bologna, whose age is unknown. She dresses very open-mindedly, she has a fleshless, springtimelike face, but pursues masculine activities in real life: financial transactions, art dealings. She has ten phone numbers with as many secretaries answering them. Each secretary records Fides's monotonous little voice, which rattles off the rosary of numbers of the other secretaries, breaking up a day into deadlines only brief minutes apart. Looking for Fides means penetrating a hypnotic mathematical and temporal universe, in which one can be imprisoned forever. In the movie, she plays the fine arts teacher. After depositing a nosegay on the desk and hanging her umbrella on the hatstand, Fides sits down and ecstatically announces: "Today, I'm going to speak to you about the great artist Giotto!"

Then she leans back behind the desk, gently disappearing. Fides has vanished that way some fifty times. And each time, Fellini has cried out, amiably and ferociously: "Stay there, Fides!" But never once has she asked about the reason for that senseless disappearance. Because the thermos of cappuccino was scheduled only for the next day.

As impassive as a tortoise behind his dark glasses (the brightest note in that inert darkness), the science teacher doesn't feel so well today. He was supposed to tell the students about the motion of a pendulum, but the lesson has unhinged his mind. And so he merely and humbly tells the students about it, albeit with slightly maniacal insistence: "I have to heal! I have to heal!

I feel something so heavy, so heavy in the middle of my head. I stop here. . . . I stop there. . . . And I have to count up to three hundred at the top of my lungs. It's crazy! It's crazy!"

"Piss-pace! Piss-pace! You're nuts! Piss-pace! Piss-pace! Janitor! Piss-pace! Piss-pace! Janitor!"

It's not a coded message, nor is it the disrespectful parody of a grotesque military parade. It's simply the ultimate highpoint of concentration when Fellini directs an actor. It's the moment when the mathematics teacher notices the urine puddle at the feet of the student by the blackboard. Who knows, perhaps the material taught by her is what soon provokes an identical abstract indication: "Hands-ass, hands-ass, hands-ass-cock, hands-ass-cock." That happens when the teacher becomes the protagonist of Titta's erotic hallucination. She has the face of a soubrette, and it always seems to be emerging from spangles, paillettes, applause (she's even worked with Macario, the comedian), and from a decidedly horselike set of teeth. When a lovely horse's tail is sewn to the back of her skirt, the math teacher suddenly becomes more nonchalant, more secure, she demonstrates the calm and slightly disdainful hauteur of a woman who is finally at ease. Has this equine transfusion given her a more authentic dimension? The fact that she asks to take home the tail would seem to confirm that disquieting suspicion. She even has to whinny: "Hiiiiiiiiiiii!"

Fellini: "Flaunt your teeth. Flaunt your teeth when you whinny!"

The she-centaur: "As if I were smiling? Ah, but horses don't smile. . . ."

An ancient, nostalgic ability? Earlier, during the Fides scene, she smiled. Now she whinnies. But she's utterly happy.

The Italian teacher is a doctor. Excuse me. A doctor is playing the Italian teacher. He wears spectacles as thick as field glasses, but he can only make out silhouettes. In *Roma*, he had a bit part in the popular whorehouse sequence. That's why Fellini welcomed him with these words: "Are you still going to brothels?" Upon learning that the man is a doctor, he asked him, curiously: "Why do you want to be in the movies?"

The doctor: "Because I love paradox. I like to act in order to express myself, communicate. . . ."

There are a huge number of people who, to satisfy that need, insist on working again and again with Fellini. Which means that they can succeed only in a mysterious and outlandish communication. Perhaps like this: The purblind doctor, sitting behind the desk in a dismal and smelly classroom filled with lazy and insolent pupils, thunders out a dramatic poem by Alfieri: "We'll see the day — We'll see the day on which . . ." According to the script, the Italian teacher, while reciting, has to sprinkle sparkling saliva on the pupils in the front rows. The doctor does his best, risking utter dehydration. But he can't get it right. So he resigns himself to having a property man behind him, who sprays out an Alfierian excess of wetness. But what does it matter? Immersed among voices, invisible presences, the clear darkness of the reflectors, the physician, purple with inspiration, is alone no more.

The shooting of the school sequences unleashed the most furious and homicidal war of the entire project between Fellini and the actors.

Here are the most frantic points:

Fellini: "I'm going to throw myself out the window! Out the window!"

Math teacher (sincerely curious): "Why?"

Fellini: "Because I want to throw myself out the window!"

"I'm going to scratch up my entire body if you don't pay attention!"

"I'm going to chop your head off, it's no use to you anyway!"

"Maurizio [the assistant director], grab her! Otherwise I'll strangle her!"

"Don't faint anymore, there's no cognac left!"

"Don't say you understood! Don't say it! Say you didn't understand, and we can all go home!"

And the actors? I think they must have realized the whole

business was none of their business. Fellini was almost compulsively intent on personally testing another character in the film: Titta's virulent father. So they ignored his outbursts. Victims have a sixth sense for recognizing themselves.

The magnificent nobility of Lovignano.

He, the count, is a genuine nobleman from Torino, a colonel of the grenadiers. Skinny and cadaverous, he is somewhere between hunter and prey.

She, Contessina Diomira, looks like the Infanta of Spain, says Fellini. In *Roma,* she played the chambermaid in the protagonist's childhood family. A brilliant career. She smokes nervously, staring at the fire in the small *fogarazza.* A mysterious family defect has given her features the impassiveness of a rodent.

The count's sister, a decrepit nun, her hands swathed and tormented by the only living thing that possesses her: Parkinson's disease.

How much healthier are the servants: they drink, they toast their sick, mad bosses. They tell one another fairy tales in the hot glow of the flames. The fairy tales are Swedish, and they are told in Swedish by a Nordic chambermaid with heavy blue eyes. Who will ever fully know the dark, fearful power of the servants, their secrets, their rituals, their unrecognized feats of wonder? How pallid and perilous is the manifest security of the hallowed wielders of power!

The doubts, the torments, the reflections about the choice of faces. But then the fine, polished, and yet "natural" exactness of that choice. Still, paradoxically, at that point, on that level, Fellini could use any actor, even the most random face.

Gradisca and the prince.

Marcello di Falco, an impeccable, metaphysical operetta-prince has to appear worn out, used up by his abysmal thinking, by unbearable worries and angers.

Fellini: "Think of the Belgian debt . . . and also your own debts, Di Falco!"

An electrician: "They're bigger than the Belgian debts!"

Gradisca — first version (cut from the film):

Thrilled, panting, Magali Noël uncovers her breasts and whispers with utter dedication: *"Gradisca, principe!"* (Help yourself, prince!). At the same time, the camera advances toward her at a slow, regal pace. While Fellini, in his big, stolid voice, simulates the squeamish, neurotic princely allergies: "What's that? What are those things? Are they yours? But I've only just eaten!"

A strange fascination in this little town! Like the African disease. It's easy to remain its prisoner or be abandoned here. That's what happened to Chief of Staff Martignoni. Now he's a barber in Gradisca's shop. A gift from the prince? In olden times, royal highnesses gave presents to generals.

And what about Cervelli? If he was stricken with megalomania as a general, then later on, after being cured, he will become the director of the local insane asylum.

The Sermon *about* the Mount.

Fellini likes everything that's horizontal, stretched out. That's why he loves the sea. In contrast, he hates everything that's vertical, for instance mountains. Do these preferences also depend in part on his vocation as a showman? "Anything that's open, extended, empty can be used in creating things and their movements. A mountain panorama is already something complete. It looks like a finished backdrop."

Who can play the emir? The science teacher? Why not? In summers, teachers often pursue other activities, especially teachers who have "something so heavy, so heavy in my head." Or else Martignoni, the Chief of Staff/barber in the prince's retinue. This casting is slightly more hazardous because the emir and the prince with his retinue might stay in the Grand Hotel at the same time. Eventually, Fellini — almost like Maigret when he puffs up like a gigantic breathing and receptive sponge — and this is the solution — remembers Caldarola: the most emir-like emir of all emirs. A tiny and completely rotund creature, a nocturnal gnome, absentminded and vagabondish, sooth-saying and fortune-telling, and in lean times a peddler with a hairbrush and five Kleenex at once. From the dark, disquieting balloon, two big dark green eyes squint under very long lashes. His life has unusual rhythms. He sleeps two weeks at a stretch. Or else he spends his time traveling on all the buses in Rome, he makes his rounds and hangs out at certain coffeehouses and hotels, where he can show off his clairvoyant faculties. He passes his nights in the waiting rooms of stations, near certain precinct houses where he's friendly with the cops. He joins the clerks of the SIP Company, who are doing the nightshift at San Silvestro. Despite the flood of messages sent throughout Rome, the tiny magician can't be tracked down. Either he's switched off his mysterious relays, or else he's hermetically isolated in one of his recurrent hibernations. But then he appears on the morning of the appointed day, slowly hobbling and swaying up the road to Cinecittà. He is the emir, by God! And he has the calm, perfect punctuality of monarchs. For an entire day, with the turban on his head and two enormous emerald earrings dangling from his ears, Caldarola moves through the hall of the Grand Hotel, followed by bodyguards and dignitaries who are twice his size but whom he ignores with olympic cordiality. All that the minuscule emir does is to repeat, in his honeyed piping, a dreamy and obsessive sexual phobia, which, formulated in French, has utterly refined resonances: "*La différence qu'il y a entre la femme du chimpanzé et la mosquée de Bagdad*" (the difference between the chimpanzee's wife and the mosque of Bagdad).

Caldarola finds himself as the town beggar and more frequently as the humble messenger of extraordinary facts: the flight of the count's peacock through the blizzard! "Look! It's the count's peacock!" The outburst of the "Internationale" during the grim Fascist toasts — "They're playing the phonograph up there. . . ."

Begging is an irreparable condition, a perennial characteristic of the small town. So Caldarola will remain with us until the end of the movie. He'll spend days and nights deciphering hands and destinies, murmuring innocent obscenities to the women, handing out numbers to play in the lotto, but above all incessantly gobbling down endless tons of food and hectoliters of cappuccino, occasionally pushing back his black cape with a graceful movement and thus showing fat, delicate little hands.

The set of a Fellini movie is voraciously visited by cinema students, people doing dissertations on his films, psychologists, psychoanalysts, who come to see the living "creative process." Fellini: "It's as if someone sat down next to a sleeping man to see how he dreams. And from the panting, the quivering of the eyelids, the shreds of words and phrases that the dreamer mumbles confusedly, the observer tries to deduce the nature, the mechanics of the process of dreaming. . . ."

Fellini to a journalist: "I intend to go to Arabia for some of the shooting." Are we going to follow the emir who will be returning there? Fellini often fantasizes about going off with his characters, following them, spying on them, abandoning the story, the film . . . and especially the producers.

Aldina Cordini peers up to her aristocratic wooer, who is standing in the window of the schoolyard. From the courtyard of the Palazzo Lovignano, Colonia looks up toward the count and the countess. Biscein stares greedily at the concubines on the balcony of the Grand Hotel. Titta and his friends look up to the count's peacock, which is fluttering in the snow. The film frequently repeats situations in which a conversation unwinds between someone below and someone above. Generally, the camera sides with the bottom person.

Those Fascists!
Fellini to a Frenchman: "You were in the *Resistance*, you told me. You were a Partisan. . . . Well, so you can play a Fascist. . . . You know, the kind that proceeded with beatings and castor oil. . . ." (Hmm! Here, innocence turns into baiting.)

The small, sharp, gloomy face of the Frenchman, the tiny, gray, close-set eyes do not belong to any ideology. They belong to a character.

Another. With the hot, vivid eyes of a wounded and confused humanity. The kind of people who teach cinema with a stubbornness like disillusion, who speak about movies as though they were a Promised Land, a privileged geographic zone, a very specific continent ruled by absolute happiness. Ten years ago, that man confronted Fellini at his building entrance and pretended to swallow a tablet of some deadly poison, which was really only aspirin. An alarmed Fellini dragged him to a taxi and took him to the hospital. "For the entire drive, I had my head on Signor Fellini's shoulder. . . . At the hospital, I didn't feel like telling him the truth, so I had my stomach pumped out. . . ." Nothing happened (cruel Fellini). But now there he is, at the headquarters of the National Fascist Party, thrust into bestial black boots and the mournful uniform of the militia. But feverish with joy. Is Fellini all that cruel? Not really. People who live on myths don't make distinctions, and they are always the immediate victims.

In a revelry of banners, a blare of trumpets, a wild shouting of enthusiasm, the *Federale* gets off at the station of the small town, which materializes from a dense, dark, choking smoke. But the science teacher, in a black shirt like the other teachers, doesn't even cough. Undaunted, he faces the fog, authentically and deeply moved, in a genuine nostalgia that seems to make his turtlelike impassivity even more peremptory. Fellini notices this, snoops around him for a while, then starts baiting him, curious, urgent. The science teacher merely pulls out a yellowed "Petition to the Duce" from his wallet, with delicate reverence, and then he protests with irrevocable conviction: "But in those days I worked!"

Fellini: "They let *you* work? That alone would be enough to irremediably discredit the whole Fascist gang!"

The great theatrical actress, whose colleagues are Fellini's fantastic and irreplaceable favorites, doesn't feel like telling the director what she thinks. So she resorts to a dream: "And then I said to you: 'But Federico, why do you take on those assholes, who infuriate you, tire you out, and make you lose so much time?' . . . But you didn't answer. . . ."

Rushes: The stroll along the Corso.

Fellini is right when he says that in contrast to *Satyricon*, where the things to be seen were exotic, here it is the spectator's eye that is the "other." And it's precisely the subtle, intense shadow of familiarity that flits across the screen and makes vision an experience between torment and laughter, between pain and a strange, desperate solidarity.

Fellini: "Drop your hand as though the pulse were broken. . . . Now get up, go toward her slowly, with your lip stuck out, slowly but powerfully, as though your cock went all the way out to here, under the chin, and you were about to stick it in between her breasts. . . . Wonderful!"

These directions are for Gigino Penna Bianca, the town seducer: he simply has to invite an American woman to dance on the terrace of the Grand Hotel.

The philosophy teacher, adviser to the town's Party chief, is a high official in RAI (the Italian radio network), a fine and witty intellectual. But this experience has totally absorbed and confused him. He calls up daily to inquire how the shooting is going, to find out what we're filming on that day and if, perhaps . . . his presence isn't scheduled in the shooting plan. The answer is often negative, and so, on the other end of the wire, there are sad, endless, embarrassing pauses. It often happens with nonprofessionals participating in a Fellini movie that off the set they feel sick, confused, disoriented. Sooner or later, they can be seen arriving in Cinecittà with the classic excuse of the most hardened extras: namely, that they've come because they received a "call," a "message" summoning them. The RAI official, as a cultured man, tries to contain his disorientation with an awareness and a critical detachment that can indifferently produce unheard-of suggestions or subtle and literary definitions of the film. "Why not call the movie *The Gamble*? . . ."

What an exalting confusion.

I asked Caporale, one of Fellini's "favorite" actors, to write a few lines on the character he plays in the film, Giudizio:

"The role of Giudizio is beautiful for me, and I thank the maestro from the bottom of my heart for casting me in this role. These scenes are so impressive and they bring back to me the tough times of the thirties when I was in great difficulties and we had to wander around like gypsies. Today, I thank and I praise the Lord. I embody this role with loyalty, as in the time it took place. The character I play gives me joy, it is in this name 'Giudizio,' and working with Maestro Fellini, that I am now getting known throughout the world of show business. Caporale."

The characters necessary in the film are practically all inhabitants of the town. Hence, every repetition, fact, or situation bring up the same dramatic doubts: which characters will be present and which will not? Often, Fellini's choices and exclusions have the inscrutable chanciness of life.

Or else a character without an identity acquires one suddenly. Discussion with the assistant directors.

Fellini: "In the Rex sequence, remember to include the daughter of the community scribe."

Amazed chorus of assistants: "Who is the daughter of the community scribe?"

Fellini, equally astounded: "Polini! Come on! Didn't you know that Polini is the daughter of the community scribe?"

A strenuous day. All the townfolk have been abandoned at sea for the entire day, without eating, without drinking, without stretching their legs, floating along on frail boats. A more exhausting and dangerous wait than the one forty years ago for the real Rex. When the shooting was done, there was a rollcall to make sure that no one had gone down or floated off to Sardegna.

Fellini, lost in thought: "Tomorrow is the funeral of Zanin's mother. . . . Can you imagine, I don't care about the funeral of

gali Noël (Gradisca) with Bruno Zanin (Titta) in *Amarcord*

The *Rex* in *Amarcord,* in the big swimming pool at Cinecittà

Pataca, drawn by Fellini

asant woman in *Amarcord,* drawn by Fellini

Ciccio Ingrassia as the crazy uncle (left) in *Amarcord*

The dream wedding of the two young Fascists

pino Janigro as the grandfather in *Amarcord*

Fellini with Magali Noël on the set of *Amarcord*

Zanin's mother. . . . Oh well. Who knows what I'll do. . . ."

Tomorrow, they'll be shooting the funeral of Titta's mother. Bruno Zanin is simply playing the part of Titta. What a bizarre, calculated precaution to conjure away any excessive and compromising participation.

A consultation.

The town broker is an ex-monk. How did he get into the movies? . . . "Well, I was in a rotisserie, and this guy who hires extras came over to me. . . ." A victorious temptation by the devil, it would seem. Given his former activities, he is asked to organize the ceremony of the funeral. Here are the various phases:

First:

Fellini   "Does the priest walk in front or in back of the hearse?"

Broker   (*secure*) "In back. The priest always walks in back."

Fellini   "But if I remember correctly, he walked in front. . . ."

Broker   (*hurriedly*) "At funerals. Yes, at funerals. At funerals, he walked in front."

Fellini   "And what's this? Isn't this a funeral?"

Broker   (*with the imperturbable calm of absolute conviction*) "Then he walks in back. At funerals, the priest always walks in back. Yes, yes. He's always in back."

Fellini   "And yet I still have the impression that he walked in front. . . ."

Broker   (*lightning-fast and serene*) "Certainly. Except at funerals. At funerals, the priest always walks in back."

Second:

Fellini   "How does the coffin come out of the church? Without the flowers? Without the garlands?"

Broker   (*cautious*) "It all depends. It comes out with the garlands —"

Interruption by the chief engineer in his quick booming voice:

"The coffin leaves the church bare and naked."

Fellini   "Well?"

Broker   (*very swift*) "It comes out bare and naked."

Fellini   "But weren't you just saying that it comes out with the garlands?"

Broker   (*with a sudden, rapid compliance*) "Of course! It comes out with the garlands. You can see that the deceased was very popular. . . . All those flowers. . . ."

Third:

Fellini   "Where does the band walk? In front or in back of the hearse?"

Broker (*suspicious*) "It all depends. . . ."
Fellini "On what?"
Broker (*logical, unimpeachable*) "On whether it's in front or
        in back."

It's too bad that ultimately all the voluntary suggestions of the
adviser were ignored. The result would have been an unforgettable funeral. As unforgettable as the broker's memories:

"The particular sensations of mystical devotion that I felt led
me to offer advice on the scene, which made my Latin liturgical
responses more lively and more active. Thus my deeply emotional participation in that funeral ceremony constituted the
most beautiful, most suggestive, and most incomparable moments of my cinematic activity: moments that shall remain truly
imprinted on my mind with an indelible stamp, with such a
force that they contributed to my final decision to forgo any
other activity in favor of the cinema."

The broker also has ecstatic recollections of his own character:
"Something that deserves special mention is my participation in
the scene that was filmed in the town of Ostia Lido, where I repeatedly drove down the main street in an ancient automobile
of that era. I was seated in front, next to the driver, in a close-
up, with my nose against the windshield, while Maestro Fellini,
directing the scene, kept calling my name and constantly asking
me to come more into view. And I was exceedingly proud and
content because of that treatment and because of Fellini's special consideration, for I was aware that this was truly a marvelously beautiful 'close-up,' highly important and totally worthy of
the name."

But brutally cut from the film.

And a metaphysical incarnation promptly revealed itself in
the bank employee sent for the weekly inspection of the *Amarcord* rushes. He was tall, skinny, his hair was smooth and white,
his face bony. Altogether, he had a humble, vaguely confused,
and neurotic courtliness. By sheer accident, for reasons that I
no longer recall but that I now feel were due to some fateful
pertinence, I was asked to accompany the bank employee to the
showing. We sat down on the very comfortable divan at the

back of a small, warm, elegant room. All at once, the lights
went out, and in the silence that was filled with the metallic
humming of the projector, the images of the school sequences
began flitting across the screen. I was quiet and attentive.

Suddenly, without looking at me, the bank man made a
frankly eulogizing comment about the robustness of my physical
makeup. He said that I reminded him of a Swiss friend, a
woman in her fifties, who lifted weights every day in order to
keep in shape. I smiled embarrassedly, not so much because of
the unusual nature of the compliment, but because I couldn't
think of any more-or-less natural response. Undaunted by my
hesitant silence, the reckless bank man asked me, with a peculiar and almost anxious curiosity, what sport I practiced or
would like to practice. From the very start, he had been
squirming and fidgeting on the divan, changing his position,
hunting about in his briefcase, checking the time by holding up
his watch to the light from the screen. In reply to his question
about my sports activities, I diligently said that I liked to swim,
and that in high school I had done well with discus throwing in
student contests. My interlocutor's face lit up with a decidedly
self-complacent enthusiasm, not so much for the precision — I
felt — as for the reality of his prediction. Hmm, I reflected to
myself, the job of viewing every frame of every rush of countless films can ultimately become unbearable. Everyone has the
right to stave off boredom and monotony in any way. The next
question hardly left me time to consider that my companion's
way of fighting boredom was none too common. It was quite
elaborate and unforeseeable:

"Have you ever arm-wrestled?"

I thought seriously for a moment, then answered: "Yes . . .
sometimes. With friends. . . . Just for fun. . . ."

In the penumbra, my guest's voice resounded, secure, satisfied: "And I bet you were always the winner."

I knew he'd be disappointed. But at this point, any effort at
hedging would be unacceptably ridiculous. "No, not always.
Sometimes I won, sometimes I lost. . . . It depends on my opponent. . . ."

He was disappointed. But only for an instant. At bottom, the realism of my admission, although unexciting, was nevertheless concrete and credible. It was enough to arouse the elderly bank employee's interest in that disquieting conversation.

On the screen, the fine arts teacher was ecstatically telling the pupils about Giotto's fundamental discovery: "Perrr-speccccc-tive!" Suddenly she dunked the cookie into her light coffee with a flick of childish voraciousness. It was exactly at this moment that my friend formulated his marvelous, metaphysical proposition:

"Would you like to arm-wrestle with me?"

It was clear that a very ordinary boredom did not suffice to explain or justify. In a fraction of a second, I recited all of Leopardi's *Tedium Vitae* to myself — to a point of forgetful and catatonic immobility. But I couldn't succeed in identifying, in classifying what was happening. So I abandoned myself to avid participation. It was only out of a sense of duty that I hazarded: "You mean . . . right now?"

The man who was now my partner replied impatiently but kindly: "Yes, of course. Since we'll be here for two hours, it could be an amusing way of passing the time!"

We got up simultaneously from the divan and began hunting about in the darkness for a horizontal plane that would be suitable for that incredible challenge. In a corner, half-concealed within a niche, there was a square crystal table some thirty centimers high. I might have ignored it, but I was sparked by a perplexed loyalty and perhaps by a fear that everything would come to a standstill because of some wretched contretemps. On the other hand, I couldn't beat my companion in an initiative that had come from him by proposing that the table was inadequate. So I merely said with nonchalance: "There's this table, but it's too low."

The rejoinder came instantly: "No it's not. We could sit on the floor. . . ."

The soft carpet on the floor seemed the most sensible of invitations, the most logical of reasons, almost a mandatory imposition to sit down. So we sat down. On the floor. Placing our elbows on the crystal plane and enlacing our hands. The bank employee's hand was soft, cold, and a bit sweaty. For an instant, I pictured someone coming in at that moment, I even hoped it might be the producer, that is to say, the individual whose arrogant power depended exclusively on the bank that had sent us this bizarre employee and that was providing the cash necessary for making the film. I began to press my adversary's arm down. His resistance was slight. I recalled with a smile that I had thought it might be better to let the man win. Who knows? A defeat might have made him look askance at *Amarcord* and give negative or delaying reports to his superiors. But I promptly realized that his resistance was not so much frail as complying. The man *wanted* to be beaten, conquered, mortified. What happened next confirmed that beyond any doubt. With an utterly natural gesture, he had slipped his other hand into his trouser pocket, and now a jingling of keys could be heard from there. The rhythm was more and more accelerated. What could I do? The ghost of Baron Sacher-Masoch enjoyed my full solidarity. Moreover, it would have been exceedingly rude or idiotic on my part to simulate a repugnance that I did not really feel or a breeding whose sense and laws I did not know. Furthermore, the raptus I was confronted with was restrained by such a civil, such an unembarrassed and fastidious, such an absolutely unobscene impassiveness that in an impulse of generosity I decided to shift from solidarity to collaboration. With a knowing and supportive slowness, I bent down my voluntary victim's arm. The back of his hand touched the crystal of the table. The jingling of the keys halted, gently. On the screen, Titta's grandfather was moving through the fog, alarmed and anxious. In the little room, I heard only the abstract hum of the projector, but I knew that at this moment, the grandfather was calling: "Gina! Gina!"

Merely an impression of the film: It seems to me that the splendid formal carelessness in *Amarcord* has the most moving and vivid congruence with the narrated material. The singular stylistic chastity makes me think of an author who — in the sense of identification — believes more in what he tells than in himself. In one of his swift appearances in the office of the assistant directors, Fellini blinked at the affirmation that an author

can believe more in what he does than in himself. According to
Fellini, it's exactly the other way around: he believes more in
himself, even exclusively in himself. The result was a di-
vergence of opinions that was never resolved. It was irreparable, irreconcilable. For the person enjoying a work, it is the
result that counts. And the more notable the result, the more it
becomes the direct element, the more the author tends to vanish (paradoxically) and be integrated in the result. But it's different for the author. It can't help being different. A silkworm
produces silk not because it believes in it, but because it exists.
That's all it can believe in.

Amarcord too ends in the desolation of Focene. Like *Satyricon*. This time too: a rite, a departure.

Because of the instability of the weather — sun, grayness,
rain — Fellini begins shooting the sequence again each time at
the point at which it was interrupted and in the version of the
meteorological whim of the moment. . . . "In this way, *Amarcord* never saw the light, because today, twenty years later,
Fellini and his troop are still celebrating Gradisca's marriage
without reaching the end. An invincible spell imprisons them in
the thornbushes and sand and wind."

What difference is there between that impossible possibility
and Fellini's equally impossible but sincere fantasy when he
repeats: "Why print the material that's been shot? Isn't it
enough just to shoot it?"

"Asabasiv" is the mysterious word that the photographer in
Amarcord utters before fixing the people and events of the town
on his camera plate. To discourage any questions or hypotheses
about that, Fellini has explained in a footnote in the script that
"Asabasiv" is the word used by the ancient inhabitants of Romagna's hinterland for a certain hour of the day. Hence, the
perplexed note goes on, it is not clear why the photographer
uses that word at any moment, for any hour of the day. Fellini's
meticulous gloss is clearly provocative, for it is pure invention,
an innocent, joking revenge on empty erudition. But perhaps
the photographer isn't all wrong: the moment in which reality is

translated into its own image, the instant in which life becomes its own effigy, requires a warning that is at least as arcane as the event that it announces is prodigious.

Erudition for erudition's sake: The Masai, a group in Central Africa, have a taboo on any type of image that depicts them, because they consider it a vampirelike sucking of their vitality, a fearful attack on the very existence of the model. If this dark presentiment of the Masai were exact, we could know with certainty whether reality actually dies out in that absorbing parallel life, that monstrous reflecting fetish that is its own image, spreading in all formulas and on all levels. In that gray, spectral, and mechanical backdrop, we could confirm the suspicion — the extreme test of his topicality, the total congruence of the director and his time — that Fellini, a man who has exhausted himself and his life in images, doesn't actually exist.

31

Casanova Said to Fellini:
"Signore, Use the Polite Form with Me!"

"FELLINI'S MAKING CASANOVA!"

The announcement promptly offered the charismatic and satisfying validity of a fact of destiny, the contagious élan of a collective effort, the arrogant exuberance of a battle that's already been won.

"DINO DE LAURENTIIS IS PRODUCING FELLINI'S CASANOVA!"

The sodality — almost a wistful mythical trinity of miracles — seemed to unleash the irreparable vigor of an avalanche, displayed the iconographic solemnity of a *missa cantata*, and even apparently aroused the sophisticated excitement of obvious risk. On the one side, the legend of a man dedicated to the most unbridled economic profligacy, yet knowing himself to be submissive and yielding only to the concrete demands of his work. On the other side, a typically Italian financial soundness, i.e., feeding on its own exorbitant losses. But isn't De Laurentiis the builder of pyramids, of cinematic Great Walls of China? Like *The Bible, War and Peace, Waterloo?* At the center, a theme as monumental and universal as the Punic Wars or *The Master of Ballantrae.* Hence, the object of bewildered or fascinated hypotheses and prognoses.

The start of preparations for the film was likewise impeccably efficient: very central offices, right near Termini Station, guaranteed the functional access to a recruiting area. And they punctually became permanent bivouacs, encampments crowded with physical persons or epistolary ghosts — those always wretched and marvelous "undersigned" who "hope to enter the motion-picture world because movies are in my blood." Talent scouts, unleashed like hired assassins, roamed the length and breadth of Europe, their pockets holding detailed descriptions of all the chief characters in the film.

A set-design laboratory was fitted out, and it immediately had the sinister and villainous look of the spearhead troop of an era, a century — the *settecento,* the eighteenth century. Then came a breakneck series of script scrutinies, budgetary estimates, working plans: battalions of numbers, days, places, people cascaded upon ever-new and ever-urgent settlements.

In that triumphant and pragmatic apparatus, in that dizzying mélange, in which the industrial machine reverberates in Luna Park, the only false note, the only detail that didn't fit in was: Fellini. Yet Fellini was the keynote, the fundamental detail — the reality!

The director came to his new offices with his photographic archive, a package of extra-strong bond, and colored Magic Markers. Irritated and ironic, he promptly disowned the feverish multinational society that welcomed him: "One of these days, I'm going to make myself a bicycle cart like that of Biscein, the itinerant peddler in *Amarcord.* I'll put all my stuff in it, and instead of changing offices each time, I'll just peddle my way through the city from point to point."

Together with the tools of his trade, Fellini always had, with him, inside him, outside him, a profound and incurable distrust of the film. Every day, he obstinately made mountains of his distrust, a soft wall, and he barricaded himself, concealed himself behind it, listless and irritable. He emitted only the pallid attention of an invalid to the actors who came for casting. He went to Danilo Donati in the set-design department like an occasional guest, elusive and impatient, always ready to agree quickly and wearily. It was something like an extraordinary game of tarot, a state of trance evoking people and situations, which is the only way for Fellini to slowly consult and inspect the thousands of photographs in his archive. But ultimately, the tarot degenerated into the mechanical inertia of a clerical job.

With zeal and relish, however, he was the man who busied himself with tuning the false note, making the deviant detail fit in. Or with the transcendental comfort of statistics: all of Fellini's recent films, which are perhaps his most important, have been created amid alienation, intolerance, polemical detachment. Or else, by means of the indisputable syllogism into which theology often transmutes faith: if distrust and hostility are the director's feelings when approaching the film, then distrust and hostility are the proteins that the film greedily craves, the genetic code that organizes it.

Fellini's head-on collisions with the film, his sometimes embarrassing verbal brawls with *Casanova*, were the only occasion on which the director seemed to revive, to recover from the somnambulistic malaise that paralyzed him. Not only that, but his erosive meanderings on the character, the degrading comparisons, the mortifying diagnoses, the brutal insults, an inexhausted repugnance were sparked by such an image-ridden confusion, such a participating metaphorical tension, that for any listener those things became the signs of a sure gestation. For Fellini, however, it was a simple matter of virulent motives for an irremediable quarrel, an impossible birth.

Then, De Laurentiis wept. He read the script and he wept, agitated and enthusiastic. The Neapolitan producer's unsuspected, almost girlish vulnerability was moved by a screenplay that had the chilling character of an asphyxiated and repetitive pantomime. And his reaction surprised and amused Fellini. One week later, the director learned that De Laurentiis's aesthetic ecstasy was nothing but an outburst of financial eroticism.

To the producer's entranced eyes, Casanova, page by page, took on the rude, blond features of a rugby player, Robert Redford. And behind him, the male sex symbol of America during the seventies, came the alluring cortege of sirens — the major American production companies. De Laurentiis's shining, hypnotic vision (the shininess of money) struck against Fellini's malign and derisive silence. The producer begged him: "Why can't you take Redford? Listen, Fefé, he'll follow you like a puppy dog. 'Redford, fetch! Redford, sit!' You can do anything with him." The producer was beside himself: "Besides, what do you care! You can cast Redford and then stick a mask on him. Any mask you like. Casanova's face!"

Nothing doing!

Vanquished, the producer hazarded a final remedy, an emergency solution: an airlift bringing a flock of American stars, Casanova's women, to Cinecittà? Tranquil and gathering wool, Fellini did not propose any alternatives, he made no decisions, no selections. He refused adamantly, though feeling very compassionate toward the producer, who, an innocent Sisyphus, insisted on trying to achieve some congruity between his simply amazing innate Neapolitan ruthlessness in business and his esteem and affection for his friend Fefé. However, Fefé, precisely for being an artist, is utterly alien to De Laurentiis.

De Laurentiis gave up. Consistent with his reputation as a tireless traveler, Casanova changed his home, his country, but not his director. For he wanted Fellini. The Rizzoli empire celebrated the return of the "prodigal son." Angelo, the head of the clan, had cheerfully funded *La Dolce Vita*, *8½*, *Juliet of the Spirits*. Andrea, the son, produced *Casanova*. Still cheerfully, but with the more detached cheer of a stockbroker. In Ferragosta, at his Cap-Ferrat villa, Rizzoli the publisher signed the contract between a silent dip in his pool and an indecipherable *ritornello* in a girlish falsetto ("That simple pink dress . . ."). The continuity of a dynasty was assured afterward by the embellishment of a selfsame coat of arms.

The film transferred to Cinecittà, and during that passage, it inadvertently skidded into a tunnel, a glass sphere, like the kind that used to encase domestic saints and mountain madonnas. From inside, you can still see the trees, the sky, the outer world. But the sphere soon turns out to be a magnetic field, compulsory and immobilizing, a dense, bewitching balance of a useless activity, a magician's conveyor belt, on which everything and everyone keeps moving and moving without knowing toward what.

The art direction, equipped with kilometers of plans and designs, was the heaviest feature of the film: a disjointed body that sloughed away from all the new studios made available in Cinecittà, like a clown that wants to stuff a grand piano into a suitcase. If a miracle did happen, then the shooting would have to follow an assembly-line schedule.

The only real and concrete vitality of the film was its cost, which increased visibly under the blows of inflation, devaluation, investment crises: a bladder filling up with air, with emptiness. . . .

And Fellini? The director assiduously frequented his office, an immense room with a tiny desk in a corner. And above the desk, an arrow pointing imperiously at him, Fellini himself, sitting behind the desk. The entire picture was a mute and blatant denunciation of a cataleptic state involving an immediate salvation, not *of* the film, but *by* the film, by Casanova. The picture became animate only to translate into an atrocious psychodrama: Fellini's antipathy, rancor, repugnance seemed to have embodied Casanova into a flesh-and-blood enemy whom he had to fight hand to hand, furiously, in savage, breathless rounds of catch-as-catch-can. And there were blows below the belt: the director sent another difficult and elusive person into the ring to challenge the Venetian: Mastorna. And let the best man win. Mastorna is the joker, the project that, in moments of confusion, springs up like a jack-in-the-box before the producers, who are out of their depths. But he who sings "That simple pink dress . . ." did not settle the match. He disqualified the adversary and gave Casanova the unreal resurrection of cinema.

For both Federico and Casanova, the pauses between rounds, brief armistices, worked out like this: the director tormented a slip of paper with insatiable and blasphemous sketches of his opponent. One showed an enormous behind defecating a shriveled and jaunty Casanova, who announces: "And now I'll go out and discover the world!"

The cohabitation of the incompatible couple became more and more cannibalistic, it diffused a subtle feeling of menace. Fellini abandoned his room, destroyed all material traces so as not to trigger monstrous sprints, indecent pursuits, and he sought refuge in the office of his assistants. Here, stretching out on a couch, the refugee spent entire sultry afternoons replenishing himself, with the frothy vivacity of an alarmed boy. Every so often he sent one of his assistants to spy in his room, a solitary commando in enemy territory: "Go and see if 'the prick' is there. . . ."

From now on, quite rightfully, Casanova was "the prick." An embittered direct relationship turned into an insidious little war.

Accepting the postulate that every creative event is a phenomenon of possession, Fellini had for some time been in an advanced state of possession that was, however, difficult and above all mysterious. What was it then that impeded the natural development of this event? Why did Fellini keep trying to struggle free from Casanova, often with the touchiness and good arguments of a threatened feminist? Of course, according to the director's impatient simplification, everything was reduced to the fact that no creative event was in the making. Still, the difficulties of a process were enough to exclude that absence. Fellini's intellectual and psychological resistance to the character derived from a lack of congeniality, from a legitimate antipathy toward an individual whom he saw in a certain way. But if that gap tended to become neurotic, then it virtually betrayed a symptomatic frailty, it could perhaps signify that it is not yet purged by unconscious heritages, by elements alien to those that long to differentiate themselves and that are the same and that are to be stigmatized. A psychology like that of Casanova's, which Fellini gradually shaped, was now the same as that of most Italians and hence, by a constantly neutralized corruption, it was also his. Ergo: the immoderate, irrational, almost physical fear that even a temporary identification might change into an incurable regression.

But would it be like that? Was the goal of the film really that Italian archetype deduced from Casanova? Often the deepest meaning of a Fellini film appears when the film is completed, the motives running through the shooting often turn out to be a deceptive game of Chinese boxes that furnishes paltry indications about the final result, whereas the extreme importance of that game is exclusively functional, a laboratory matter. And one of the cardinal rules of that laboratory says that Fellini's imagination is kindled and operates in unexplored areas only if attracted, provoked, protected, and mediated by familiarity: themes, situations, psychology, feelings, and resentments.

But all this is still not the crux. Fellini had conceived Casanova, that is to say, he breathed him, lived him, felt him as an extreme example of a nonexistence: once again, a chief feature of the character, that nonexistence of his, dovetailed or gravitated in that other, far more peculiar inexistence, that artist-mirror, that sponge, that zombie that the first inexistence had to receive and organize expressively. If Casanova was to be born, Fellini had no choice but to exorcise Fellini.

This is the point to set down, to narrate in some way a matter so complex and bizarre as to be particularly seductive. We were thinking about doing a "special," a filmed program. Fellini instantly went for the project with vengeful ardor: the modesty of an inevitably parasitical operation struck him as too exhausting for a querulous and boring peacock like Casanova. He hoped that our investigation would prove him right, legitimize his anti-Casanova judgments, and denounce all the putrefied sediments of a detestable myth. Or perhaps he thought he could free himself from the encumbering cocoon that he had been orgiastically trapped in for over a year, entrusting him to the mediated domicile of the "special," abandoning him like a wreck in a car dump.

Deprived of the film, Casanova settled down in the "special." But without the film, the "special" advanced in an itinerary that seemed to have no aim. Casanova and *Fellini's Casanova* pur-

sued one another, were superimposed on one another, and re-
pulsed one another in a game of conjectures, exemplifications,
diagnoses, representations, a game that was shrill and slightly
darkening. And we, who were occupied with that game for
months, and perhaps for that very reason — we ultimately re-
tained only shreds of sentences, a nervous tic, unreasonably
dilated impressions, an adjective, an attitude, an image.

The psychological and ideological premises of the "special"
were convincing on the level of costume notes, but perhaps
they were ultimately negated by the film. Certainly, that be-
wildering arabesque of a magic lantern, astir with bright and
fleeting voices, shadows, apparitions, so exactly restored that
"dizziness of the void" which stunned Fellini whenever he
faced the character of Casanova. And the light amusement of the
"special" was a kind of exhilarating precaution for containing that
vertigo.

Thus, although with the dreadful reluctance of a shipwrecked
passenger, Fellini sank deeper and deeper into a tempestuous
intimacy with Casanova. Meanwhile, we assistants inquired into
the elementary signals arriving on the surface, and in our eager
desire to decode the overall message, we froze it into the bom-
bastic conceptuality of abstractions (the same conceptuality that
is often at the source of unsuccessful creations). Fellini said:
"For me, Casanova was starting to stink. . . ." The assistants
zealously translated more or less: ". . . Taking off from the
emblematic figure of Giacomo Casanova, Fellini intends to
widen the discussion to the problems of the inauthentic, which
are always present in the works of the director from Romagna. . . ."

But the "director from Romagna," with his flair for ridiculing
silly intellectualizations by deflating them with the violent and
ambiguous hyperboles of fact, confessed one day that he had
had a secret meeting with Casanova. Whether this was imagi-
nary or merely true was an inane distinction in Fellini's strongly
metaphorized world. Things went more or less like this: Fellini
met with his friend Gustavo Rol, sensitive medium, and in Rol's
house in Torino, they organized a kind of "table" for reaching
the dead personage. The director was finally face to face with

the evoked spirit of the libertine. But this confrontation instantly turned out to be a troublesome conference for the powdered Venetian. Casanova struck up a dialogue with Fellini, calling him "Signor Goldoni" (what does he know about movies? His only vague notion of his inflexible modern auditor's profession is the theater, more precisely the exuberant theater of Goldoni). Then, squeamish, fastidious; "And please use the polite form with me!"

"That shithead of a Frenchman by adoption! That forerunner of ridiculous Fascist habits!" the director would subsequently rave.

Within less than ten seconds of utter darkness, Rol the magician filled some forty pages with the dry, tiny script of the author of the *Mémoires*. At the end of the angry rendezvous, Fellini saw something materialize in his jacket pocket: an unequivocal calling card of the seducer, with some advice on sexual hygiene personally addressed to Fellini: "Never on your feet. Never after eating." The director went back to Rome, depressed and ready to give up (if he possibly could have been more of either) after that esoteric confirmation of his doubts: there it was, the hysterical formalism of the parvenu and the impudent graphomaniac winding up in the beckoning jostle of the young steer who was lavishing amorous connivances.

Meanwhile, back in Cinecittà, Clemente Fracassi, the frugal vice-president of Rizzoli Films and the hypertense organizer of *Casanova*, a fine, intelligent man, and a highly competent movie man, albeit incurably restrained by a total ideological pessimism about the present state of the world, was going through the actual data of the situation to show Fellini's dangerous incapacity and the hazardous financial volume of the film, the objective occasion for a feast of his *tedium vitae*.

The extreme attempt at seizing the project by the hair, so to speak, i.e., compelling Cinecittà to reduce the costs of studios and constructions, was resolved in an ill-omened blackmail: they employed the ruse of dismantling offices and laboratories, of having people and apparatuses abandon Cinecittà. But, as it happened, this carefree weekend break became a heavy vacation.

And the cast of the film? Leaving aside the other characters, who was going to play Giacomo Casanova? That likable Canadian actor, Donald Sutherland, a dark horse who seemed to emerge from improbable hearsay, gradually solidifying through the sheer repetition of his name, sent Fellini bunches of red roses accompanied by declarations of love. On the other hand, Gian Maria Volonté, a guerrilla actor, whom the director seemed more seriously interested in, asked for four hundred million lire without further ado. Considering that Volonté is a deeply committed performer (he often works gratis or nearly so for political movies), the enormous sum seemed to quake with vindictive disdain or even dissent from a prestigious but apolitical project. And perhaps the actor was erring on the side of negligence: even the revolution has its "Trojan horses" and someone sent one out for Fellini.

With all accounts at hand, and punctiliously specified, the film's budget soared to a dizzying height of five billion lire. Excluding the paid interest. The occult song "That simple pink dress . . ." did not stop all at once, but it did die out in jerks of loud perplexity. Andrea Rizzoli, after hesitations, repentances for having hesitated, and then new doubts, finally decided not to make *Casanova*. And, a morbid totem, impatient with earthly intrigues and, above all, explanations, he left both up to his administrative delegates.

Expelling Fellini's film (a risk that seemed to have no support on paper) from the highly industrialized entrepreneurial network of Rizzoli Films unexpectedly vindicated some surprising absolutions. And then the overabundant district heads of distribution, headstrong managers, dry retailers covered with cashmere, while nimbly seizing the minimum guarantees already paid, shook their heads with inconsolable sadness, haphazardly simulating cunning aesthetic sorcerers: "It's a graveyard film." But then someone restored a decent equilibrium with a far more convincing immediacy: "There's no cunt." In regard to Casanova's women, wasn't it Fellini who excluded all desirability by talking about venerable old ladies, hunchbacks, giantesses, transvestites, hemophiliacs?

Together with the inseparable photo archives, the package of

extra-strong bond, and the colored Magic Markers, Fellini transferred to his little office on Via Sistina. Since the blinds were
always drawn, he had to keep a pair of discreet lamps lit during
the day. The storm windows did not keep out the noise from
the street, they merely seemed to conceptualize it. A harassing
defect in the electricity knocked out the radiators at briefer and
briefer intervals, so that a scarf and a woolen hat became necessary conditions of survival. The cushions on the armchair and
the couch were turned against the backs in endless rearrange-
ment.

And here, in this nocturnal exile, Fellini set up his camp.
Never by himself: gone was the diaphragm of *Fellini's Casanova*, which made for an extreme cohabitation, almost metaphysical — an absolute ownership. Days and hours, facts and objects, feelings and thoughts were dark fragments gravitating in a
timorous solitude of Siamese twins. The director's negating fe-
rocity, his refusal, his ostracism were damaged by this epithelial
companion of his, they remained unflagging, they were pathological residues now subordinated to his obsession. If at first the
presence of the film tamed that devastating viscerality in a still
conceivable dissent, now, dislocated from reasons and occasion,
it was now tinged with an imperceptible dismay, which sent
Fellini back to less decipherable business, to unknown necessities.

Casanova was everywhere and in everything. A sudden escape or a constant reference in conversations. A mocking spectator of the director's convictlike daydreams when losing all
patience with his lawyers because "within two weeks I want to
be free to start another film." A Jonah, a criminal, a pernicious
germ in a rich list of mishaps: difficulties, quarrels, thefts, dis-
eases, swooping down haphazardly in the entourage that Fellini
was putting off with the unhealthiness of a bookmaker. Impul-
sion, mental material that populates the dreams of catastrophes,
mutilations, gray deadlocks: an anguishing nocturnal map of
which Fellini became a patient, satisfied daytime extension.

Casanova haunted even other people's dreams, he visited
friends at night, even far away. A Swiss lady telephoned: "Hi,

Federico, listen, before leaving I had a dream. I dreamed I was in a theater, and a severe voice said to me: 'A homosexual cannot do an opera.' So I argued with that voice to defend the homosexual. But the voice kept saying: 'No, for an opera, the audience must have the impression that a real kiss between the couple (the ones singing the duet) could be possible.' I think that the homosexual is you, and the opera would be *Casanova*, because I once even wrote to you that I saw it as an opera."

The libertine, inventor of the game of lotto and deviser of hairsplitting speculations, produced unforeseen alliances, insinuated enormous candidates for financing the film: Montedison, Gianni Agnelli, UNICEF, the UN fund for (starving) children.

UNICEF and Casanova? The unheard-of partnership surprised and embarrassed Fellini. But his embarrassment broke into uneasy irony when, during a meal in a sophisticated Roman restaurant, upsetting pictures and *risotto al tartuffo, boeuf bourguignon* and horrifying statistics, things deteriorated in a furious burst of proselytism and gastric juices.

But, more than anything, Casnova found a nook in a sort of constant nervous vibration that could reach heights of irritating comedy. In regard to the things and people surrounding him, the things he read, the sights and spectacles he saw, Fellini manifested a radical, almost hormonal dissidence, and we can credit this to an impatient critical health. But things started degenerating and losing their shapes of abnormal conflict, when in the most run-of-the-mill situations, in the most casual conversations, in regard to the most irrelevant opinions, notions, statements, as may be suggested by a restaurant or the idea of a stroll, Fellini exhibited a furious intolerance, which didn't smack of or furnish reasons. But the matter became a sort of unrestrainable negative fibrillation when the interlocutor couldn't formulate his thoughts or plans without instant and furious denials. One can think of sort of a reverse analogy: the amusing counterpoint between Petrolini's Nero and his public when the quick repartee of bravos and thank-yous at first proceeds with meditated tranquility, then continues frantically into a crisscross, an anticipation, and wild scramble of roles and times. In Fellini, all this was ultimately made ambiguous and delirious by a spiteful and playful awareness.

The fact that Casanova could become such a torment for Fellini, such a waste of time and energy, reflects classic mechanisms in Fellinian phenomenology. If an artist's creativity, even when producing ideological contents, is always and exclusively nourished by corresponding emotional values, then the point of view, the feeling of a film eventually becomes a state, an existential commitment that involves him totally, finalizing even the most deep-seated and autonomous habits, moods, and facts. So much so that Fellini could realistically trace the profound phases of his life in the simple chronology of his films. Casanova's particularly striking features derive from the anomalous fact that was at their basis for a long time. This time it was as if the film — Casanova's character in negative — had distilled a health so opulent and venomous as to intoxicate the very creative élan that was supposed to nourish it. It seemed as if Fellini and the film's personage could not coincide either by abandoning identity or according to the rules of identification. They only succeeded in mingling together, contaminating each other, wallowing hysterically in a zone that was heavy with inconclusive impulses. For a long time, no relationship of vital metabolism came about between the two of them; there was only an inert, unproductive consistency. With an equation that was decidedly elementary but that rationalized an asphyxiating mental tautology, Fellini kept complaining: "I don't like Casanova, he irritates me, he repels me, he depresses me. That's why I don't like the film, and the thought of having to make it infuriates me, I feel so embarrassed and ill at ease that I just can't really do it."

The irritation and repuganance caused by the character were hardly the kind of feelings to stoke an imagination — however corrosive and destructive it might be. Instead, those feelings were mechanically reproduced in a passive private disgust, an opaque, realistic pathology. As luck would have it, the entire situation broke up into complex and unforeseeable resources. One of these was that no sooner had the director's meticulous exorcism put the film off indefinitely than Fellini was ready to take a deep breath and start all over again. As asphyxiating as it was, the extraordinary critical tautology, which had ignited Fellini's imagination just a while back, slackened into a potent and constructive flux, and it did not matter that Fellini was even more exhausted and excluded.

And now Alberto Grimaldi was to fish out Casanova from such an anguishing and confused topology: the same producer who had been a midwife for another forbidden voyage, *Satyricon*. Grimaldi's reasons for making the film were certainly quite different. But the fact remains that a predestination is composed of coincidences, not reasons. According to the apparently gratuitous outline of a mandala, Fellini returned to Cinecittà with his photo archives, his package of extra-strong bond, and his colored Magic Markers. He was afflicted with a dry, nervous cough: "It's the air, the unbreathable air . . . yes, the unbreathable air of Casanova!" After his latest spasmodic tremors, Fellini abandoned himself for the first time to a chaste resignation. His qualms, oppositions, an inextirpable biological hostility did not stop, but they were liberated in a verbal extroversion that supported them without exhausting them. "It's like being at the bottom of a mine, or in a prison. It's better to be still and not move, because the more you move, the worse it gets." The film was gradually to reach such dimensions as to fill out Fellini's days with a feverish, interrupted commitment. But there are certain broad and irremovable kinds of concentration that children are capable of in the most chaotic situations. And in the same way, the director maintained an obsessive feeling of constriction in his own work. A feeling that can be ascribed indifferently to the servitude in several horrible cases of the artist or to the condition of imprisonment, mutilation, heartrending self-separation of *Fellini's Casanova*.